# Short Stories from Down Under

Model Interpretations
by Arthur Kutsch

Ernst Klett Verlag
Stuttgart Düsseldorf Leipzig

# Contents

# Introduction

The predominance of Great Britain and North America in the English lessons at German schools has for a long time impeded the breakthrough of Australia, the smallest continent but the sixth largest country on Earth. The exotic background, the multicultural society, the history, and the literature of this English-speaking country have not yet been adequately opened up for students of English. However, they will surely be a welcome motivational factor for young people.

Meanwhile the world 'has become smaller', for on the one hand, the flight duration over a distance of about 20,000 km between Europe and Australia has constantly been reduced and, on the other hand, the rapid development of the electronic communication media has put an end to the 'tyranny of distance'. Today even authentic material from overseas is accessible to everybody by internet, and the increasing number of exchange visits and the growing interest in travelling to Australia, have all contributed to making 'Down Under' more and more popular with students.

This collection of short stories takes this encouraging development into account by presenting short stories dealing with scenes from urban, rural and Aboriginal life in Australia. Several principles have been decisive for the selection of the stories. First and foremost, it was necessary to choose stories that are likely to arouse young people's interest, to serve as subjects of discussion, and maybe motivate them to delve more thoroughly into Australian literature.

Secondly, the stories have been chosen because the writers are all renowned and skilful experts of their craft, each having his/her personal style and themes.

Thirdly, the stories offer a great variety of subject matter and of narrative modes.

Finally, they are intended to represent different aspects of Australian life. It goes without saying that the sequence should be regarded simply as a guideline, for each story is a homogeneous whole and the teacher or the students can make their own selection. This is why the Introduction to the Student's Book gives a short characterization of each story.

Besides the linguistic gain provided by the reading of the short stories, they will contribute to a more profound insight into the culture and history of Australia as well as the problems the country has to cope with today.

The *Model Interpretations* offer an interpretation of each short story including a plot outline. The Teaching Units suggest various teaching and learning methods such as pair/group work and individual assignments, blackboard sketches or diagrams, stimuli for discussion in class, research work on the internet, and, finally, home assignments which include a stage-script and plot-outlines both in oral and in written form.

Though the Teaching Units present many possible approaches to each story they are meant merely as a guideline. The decision as to which priorities are to be set, or how many lessons are needed for each unit, depends on the abilities and interests of the students and is therefore ultimately left to the teacher her / himself.

## Background literature

Allen, Walter. *The Short Story in English*. Oxford, 1981.

*Aspects of Australian Fiction*. Alan Brissenden, ed. Western Australia: University of Western Australia Press, 1990.

Lois, Foster and David, Stockley. *Australian Multiculturalism. A Documentary History and Critique.* Multilingual Matters 37. Clevedon, 1988.

*The Oxford Companion to Australian Literature*. W.H. Wilde, Joy Hooton and Barry Andrews, eds. Melbourne: OUP, 1942.

*The Oxford History of Australia*. Geoffrey Bolton, gen. ed. (5 vols.). Melbourne: OUP, 1986–90.

*The Oxford Literary History of Australia*. Bruce Bennett, Jennifer Strauss and Chris Wallace-Crabbe, eds. Melbourne: OUP, 1998.

*Penguin New Literary History of Australia*. Laurie Hergenhan, ed. Ringwood, Victoria: Penguin, 1988.

Shoemaker, Adam. *Black Words White Page: Aboriginal Literature 1929–1988*. St. Lucia: University of Queensland Press, 1989.

Walker, W. *Australian Literature (1864)*. Facsimile edited by Victor Crittenden. Canberra: The Mulini Press, 1996.

Tim Winton

# Neighbours

## Interpretation and Teaching Notes

### Introductory Information

*"In my stories I'm trying to render the commonplace worthy of attention.And then to have it looked at anew – and hopefully bring from that some kind of search for meaning."* (Tim Winton, 1987)[1]

Though Australia is a classical immigration country its population was quite homogeneous until the Second World War. The majority of Australians were of British heritage or had come from other European countries, and only a minority of the total population were non-white. Besides about 150,000 Aborigines, there were a few Asians, e.g. Chinese Australians, the descendants of Chinese coolies and gold-diggers who had come to Australia during the gold rush in the middle of the 19th century. After the Second World War the Australian government encouraged immigration from other European countries by extending government aid to both European and British migrants. Australia's continuing immigration programme after 1945 had an important impact on the Anglo-Celtic tradition. The introduction of non-English speaking people produced a more diverse population. But in 1973 this White Australian policy was abandoned, and the result was a significant intake from Asia. Today Australia is a multicultural society. There is a Special Broadcasting Service (SBS) providing a multilingual television and radio service; and in 1989 the Government presented a $20 million programme which aimed at acknowledging that Australian society was multicultural by offering support measures such as English language programmes for non-English speaking Australians. This gave rise to a new wave of non-English speaking immigrants. In 1996, for example, almost 7.6% of the immigrants came from China, 4.8% from Vietnam, 4.6% from Hong Kong, 4.4% from India, 3.9% from the Philippines, 3.2% from South Africa, 3.2% from Bosnia and

[1] In: Salter,Owen. "Suspicion of Hope in a Chaotic World", *On Being*, June, 1987, p. 8.

Herzegovina, 3.1% from Yugoslavia, and 2.2% from Sri Lanka.[2] In his opening address to the Global Cultural Diversity Conference in Sydney in April 1995 the Australian Prime Minister, Paul Keating, admitted that through the experience of multiculturalism Australia had learnt a lot about the management of cultural diversity: "We like to think that we might have in our modern nationhood at least some of the elements of a 21st century model – diversity, tolerance, openness and worldliness within the boundaries of national purpose and cohesion."[3]

In the last decade the total population has increased from 17,100,000 in 1990 to 18,600,000 in 2000, but only 15% of them live in rural areas. The majority of migrants to Australia has settled in the big cities, and this fact forms the background to Tim Winton's short story "Neighbours".

A newly married Australian couple have moved to a small house in the part of a city where the streets are full of European immigrants. With a Macedonian family next door on the left and a Polish widower on the right they "feel like sojourners in a foreign land" (**6**,3). First, they are shocked by the unusual behaviour of their neighbours, their activities and their shouting and screaming. It takes "six months for the newcomers to comprehend the fact that their neighbours [are] not murdering each other, merely talking" (**6**,15ff.). On the other hand, the Macedonians raise "eyebrows at the late hour at which the newcomers [rise] in the mornings" (**6**,21f.). Moreover, there is no doubt that they disapprove of the young man's staying home to write a thesis "on the development of the twentieth century novel" (**7**,19f.) while his wife goes out to work. Accustomed to the anonymity in the expansive outer suburbs where the newly-weds had grown up, they are astonished and even resentful when their neighbours constantly interfere with their work in the garden by assisting them in word and deed without being asked. In the course of time, however, the young couple find "themseves smiling back at the neighbours" (**7**,17), offering them vegetables and taking "gifts of grappa and firewood" (**7**,18) in return. One day they are stunned when the young wife learns that she is expecting a baby, for they had not planned on a pregnancy so early. When their neighbours become aware of the young wife's pregnancy, they smile "tirelessly at them" (**8**,10f.) and express their sympathy for the woman's situation by giving her small presents, offering names for the baby or even knitting a baby suit,

---

2 From: Britannica World Data "Australia" in: "1997 Britannica Book of the Year", p. 552.

3 Taken from: www.immi.gov.au/multicultural/confer/speech2b.htm

"complete with booties and beanie" (**8**,16f.). When labour starts all of a sudden the young husband stops working at his thesis. Going outside to fetch wood for the stove he sees "in the last light of the day, the faces at each fence" (**8**,29). The Macedonians are waving and calling out their best wishes. In the early morning the wife gives birth to a healthy boy. Hearing shouting outside, the young father goes to the back door. The Macedonian family, "a small queue of bleary faces" (**9**,16) behind their fence, are cheering. Overwhelmed by the emotions that had surged up in him when he witnessed the birth of his child and experiencing now the enthusiasm of his neighbours, the young man begins to weep as he realizes that his occupation with "the twentieth century novel had not prepared him for this" (**9**,17f.).

The story is told by a third-person observer / narrator in a cool and detached tone. However, there are moments when his humour becomes apparent: for example, "It took six months for the newcomers to comprehend the fact that their neighbours were not murdering each other, merely talking" (**6**,15ff.). Both the use of the impersonal third-person narrator and the fact that the characters are neither named nor depicted in detail prevent him from lapsing into sentimentality. The story shows that immigrants need not be regarded as unwanted intruders but as a social enrichment, for they bring with them a great sense of community, which seems to be lacking in contemporary urban Australia "where good neighbours [are] seldom seen and never heard" (**6**,12f.). Moreover, Winton's short narrative demonstrates that intolerance, clichés, prejudice, snobbery, and racial discrimination are based on ignorance and misunderstanding, which prevent people from living together peacefully and happily.

# Teaching Unit I

## Reading assignment

While reading the whole story at home or in class the students should take notes on the following aspects:

1. the setting of the story
2. the opening technique
3. the narrative perspective

## Comprehension check

1. Where does the young man work?
2. What is his wife's job?

3. Where had the newly-weds lived before moving into their new house?
4. Why does the boy next door make the young man nervous?
5. What did the neighbours watch fall down and how did they react?
6. Why do you think the couple's parents are shocked?
7. Why are the newly-weds stunned when the wife gets pregnant?
8. What takes the young man's breath away?
9. Why does he go outside after the birth of his son?

## The narrator and his story

### 1. The setting

*Where is the story set?*

The setting of Winton's "Neighbours" is the part of an Australian city where many European migrants have settled. Unlike in the "expansive outer suburbs where good neighbours [are] seldom seen and never heard" (**6**,12f.), the inhabitants have a highly developed sense of community. As the house the couple live in has high ceilings, paned windows and is heated with wood, and as most houses have kitchen gardens, one can conclude that it is to be found in an older part of the city. A nearby park with big Moreton Bay figs which "the young man [can] see over the rooftops" (**6**,7f.) from his study window confirms this assumption.

The events described in the story cover a period of about one and a half years, i.e. from late spring or early summer to the late autumn of the following year.

### 2. Opening technique and language

*How does the story open?*

The story opens 'in medias res' with the description of the newly-weds' strong feeling of uneasiness, caused by their new neighbourhood. Feeling "like sojourners in a foreign land" (**6**,3) the couple, who are themselves white Australians from the suburbs (cf. **6**,11ff.), are wary of their neighbours, whose unusual way of life arouses their suspicion and disapproval.

*Which factors determine the narrative tempo of the story and what is characteristic of its language?*

From the very beginning the reader realizes that the narrative tempo is fast moving. This is partly due to the narrator's use of a simple syntax which is characterized by a sequence of short sentences, consisting mostly of main clauses. This stylistic feature, however, is typical of the whole short story and reminiscent of Hemingway's paratactical style. Another element that increases the narrative rhythm is the absence of direct or reported speech. Though the story tells of the delicate relationship between the young Australian couple and their immigrant neighbours there are no dialogues. Instead, there are descriptions, some of which convey detailed information on special subjects which require technical words, such as:

1. Names of plants and vegetables: leeks, onions, cabbage, brussels sprouts, broad beans (7,3ff.), garlic cloves (7,9)
2. Special vocabulary from
   - gardening: daybreak watering, (**6**,13f.) to manure (7,2), spacing, hilling, mulching (7,5)
   - housework: to pluck, to dress (7,27), to black the stove (**8**,25)
   - building: to sink posts, to pour cement (**8**,4)
   - pregnancy and childbirth: maternity leave (**8**,1), to throw up (**8**,7), labour (**8**,24), midwife (**8**,26), contractions (**8**,33), uterus (**9**,1), pushing (**9**,5), breast (**9**,11), nipple (**9**,14), (umbilical) cord and vernix smear (**9**,12).

### 3. Point of view

*Who tells the story and through whose eyes are the events seen?*
The story is told by a third-person narrator who confines his perspective to the Australian couple, especially to that of the husband. Thus events are seen through their / his eyes and judged by them. When the young man, for example, watches the boy urinating in the street we read that he is disgusted (cf. **6**,24), or that the boy's peering through the garden fence makes him nervous (cf. **6**,27f.). Though the detached narrator relates the events in a cool tone, there are moments when his humour and irony become evident. Thus he comments that "it took six months for the newcomers to comprehend the fact that their neighbours were not murdering each other, merely talking" (**6**,15ff.), or that the future father accepts and stores packets of cigarettes at home, "not being a smoker" (**8**,12). Finally, he wonders why a man without a car builds a two-car garage (cf. **8**,20f.). However, the narrator mostly remains a neutral observer, and although he depicts how the young man matures emotionally through the birth of his child and their neighbours' sympathy and sense of community, culminating in his final insight, the story never lapses into sentimentality.

## Homework

Re-read the story taking notes on the characters and the conflict in the story.

# Teaching Unit II

## Characters and conflict

### 1. The characters

*Why are all the characters unnamed?*

While reading the short story the reader soon realizes that the narrator is not so much interested in delineating individual characters or in depicting types, but rather in representing groups of people, for no character is named and none of them is described in detail either explicitly or implicitly. Thus, the couple stand for those who have been born in Australia, whereas their neighbours represent different nationalities of immigrants, e.g. Macedonians and Poles. However, besides these differences of national origin there are also social and educational distinctions. Both are bound inevitably to lead to conflict.

*Sum up the distinguishing features of each group.*

In order to obtain a synopsis of the differences between the two groups, the students should draw up the following diagram. This can be done either together in class or in groups.

| **the couple** | **their neighbours** |
| --- | --- |
| **I. national origin** | |
| (white) Australians | immigrants |
| **II. education and social class** | |
| good college or university education | lower standard of education |
| professional class | lower social class |
| wife: nurse or doctor in hospital | probably working class |
| husband: probably post-graduate (writing his doctoral thesis) | (practical skills: carpentry and gardening / farming) |
| used to sleeping late | used to getting up early |
| **III. consequence: different modes of behaviour** | |
| *at first:* cautious / reserved / insecure / intolerant / resentful / snobbish / suspicious | *at first:* cautious / disapproving |
| *then:* try to be unprejudiced and friendly | *then:* friendly / kind / helpful / with a strong sense of community |

## 2. The conflict and its solution

*What are the stumbling-blocks that impede a harmonious coexistence between the two groups and how are they removed?*

When the new neighbours move in, the migrants display a certain distrust and disapproval, but only for a short time. On the one hand they are "cautious about the dog" (**6**,9) and on the other hand they raise "eyebrows at the late hour at which the newcomers rose in the morning" (**6**,21f.). They also frown on the young man's "staying home to write his thesis while his wife worked" (**6**,23f.). But their strong sense of community soon enables them to take steps towards good neighbourly relations. Their attempts at contact are manifold:

- giving gardening advice (7,5–9) and "a bagful of garlic cloves to plant" (7,9)
- rebuilding the henhouse (7,11–12)
- helping with the ducks (7,26–31)
- showing interest in the wife's pregnancy (**8**,9–18)
- offering "barrowfuls of woodscraps for their fire" (**8**,23)
- calling out "their best wishes" during labour (**8**,30f.)
- cheering at the fence when the baby is born (**9**,15–17).

The couple's resentment at their neighbours' way of life is much stronger than the other way round (or seems so because of the narrative perspective). They are shocked at the noises the neighbours make (**6**,13–15 + **8**,3–5), they disapprove of their disorder (**6**,17–19), resent their unwanted interference in gardening (7,5–6), find the boy's behaviour shameless and unhygienic when he urinates in the street or sprays "the cat from the back step" (**6**,25), and are irritated by his nosiness when he peers through the garden fence (cf. **6**,27f.). Their attempts at friendship are at first rather hesitant. In spite of resenting his neighbours' interference when they start gardening, the young man "takes careful note of what is said" (**7**,6f.), while his wife is "bold enough to run a hand over the child's stubble" (**7**,7f.). By autumn, however, they smile at the neighbours and offer presents (7,17f.), and in spring enjoy the communal slaughter of the ducks. But these attempts are overshadowed by new irritations and suspicions (cf. **8**,4ff.) when the young woman gets pregnant, although they are at the same time touched by the interest and the presents they receive during this period (**8**,9ff.). In the end their neighbours' solidarity during the young woman's labour and their cheering at the birth of their son is likely to put an end to the young couple's reserve and scepticism, and link the two groups in a common humanity.

The following diagram could illustrate the different phases of mutual acclimatisation:

| | | |
|---|---|---|
| **neighbours** | | |
| period of slight distrust and disapproval | offer help and advice | smile politely, exchange gifts |
| **spring/summer > autumn > late autumn/winter/spring** | | |
| **the couple** | | |
| period of distrust and misunder-standing | resent interference but accept advice | smile back and offer presents |

| | | |
|---|---|---|
| **neighbours** | | |
| cooperation and sociability | interest in the wife's pregnancy: gifts and advice | cheering at the birth of the baby |
| **late spring > summer > autumn > late autumn** | | |
| **the couple** | | |
| cooperate with neighbours but feel antagonized by Polish widower | the Australian wife feels flattered but irritated | husband's final insight |

### 3. The meaning of the story

*What is the author trying to say?*

First and foremost, the story demonstrates to its readers that intolerance, clichés, prejudice, snobbery, and racial discrimination are based on ignorance and misunderstanding and prevent people from living together peacefully and happily.

Moreover, it makes it plain to us that foreigners and migrants with their strong sense of community are a great gain to our modern urban society with its increasing anonymity.

Last but not least, the author is gently critical of intellectuals – here the husband who deals with literature as an end in itself – who are not prepared by their education for the emotions of real life.

*How does the author convey his meaning?*
With its simple syntax, its paratactical style, its absence of dialogue, and its impersonal third-person narrator, the story is reminiscent of a report. And it is precisely these stylistic characteristics, together with the fact that the characters are unnamed and thus represent typical groups not individuals, that make the story convincing and avoids a schoolmasterish tone as well as sentimentality.

## Teaching Unit III

### Post-reading activities

**1. Brainstorming:**
*a) How should we behave towards newcomers, foreigners, immigrants, minorities etc.? Find adequate adjectives.*

tolerant • unprejudiced • polite • friendly • respectful • helpful • amiable • gentle • upright • unselfish • (altruistic) • sincere • modest • thankful • humble • honest • generous • patient • sociable • kind • etc.

*b) What attempts at contact could we make with them?*

greet and address them in the street • show interest and listen to their problems • give advice • offer practical help • invite them to our homes • accept their invitations • respect their customs, peculiarities, and religion • look for information about their way of life • protect them from other people's lies, half-truths, clichés, and prejudice • learn their language • be kind to and patient with their children • etc.

**2.** *Write the author's story as seen through the eyes of the Macedonians.*

**3.** *Scan the text and find examples of prejudice and intolerance.*

Marjorie Barnard

# The Lottery

## Interpretation and Teaching Notes

### Introductory Information

Though Australian women were granted the right to vote in national and local elections as early as 1902, there were still limits on women's participation in professional life. Progress in this field was rather slow in the years that followed, for the prevailing notions still tended to confine women to their traditional roles as housewives and mothers. Finally, the slight emancipatory developments were set back by many years when the Great Depression of the 1930s struck Australia hard and imposed a degree of social misery the country had never known. For the first time population growth slowed down and emigration exceeded immigration.

"The year 1931," says J. K. Ewers, "was one of the gloomiest in Australian history [...] The economic depression, coming like a nemesis after the false prosperity of the post-war decade, reached its nadir in that year"[1]. In fact, the economic slump in the USA and other industrialized countries which followed the economic boom of the 1920s in the United States, afflicted Australia, too. It was a profoundly disturbing trauma. In Australia the rates rocketed from an average of 10% unemployment during the 1920s to more than 30% in the early 1930s. This brought poverty, hardship and hopelessness to millions of people. Mostly affected were the weaker social groups as, for example, families with children. It stands to reason that in such a bad economic situation the chances for women's jobs were very small. With the end of the crisis, this precarious situation gradually improved but the traditional gender roles still prevailed. While their husbands earned little money for their work, the wives had to make ends meet, set their personal wishes and needs aside, and were unable to save any money. But what was even worse, their chores at home were still held in low esteem. For a long time women were seldom to be seen in public bars where Australian men had a drink with their mates and talked about work, cars, etc., i.e. about

[1] Ewers, J. K. *Creative Writing in Australia*. Melbourne: Georgian House, 1945, p. 78.

everything but his wife and his family. The inferior status of women and their limited opportunities for development improved decisively in the second half of the 20th century as soon as economic conditions got better and household appliances freed women from the labour-intensive chores at home. Other positive factors were a better education for girls, and new possibilities of birth control, which led to smaller families.

"The Lottery", first published in 1943, is set in an Australian city shortly after the Great Depression. Ted Bilborough, who works in an office, has just boarded the 6.15 p.m. ferry from town which has taken him home from work for ten years, when one of his friends shakes his hand and murmurs "a few words of manly but inappropriate sympathy" (**11**,3f.), while the eyes of the other mates are focused on him. He thinks they are pulling his leg when they tell him that his wife, Grace, has won the lottery. But his doubts vanish as soon as they show him the news in the local paper which says: *First prize £5000 Last Hope Syndicate,* and that the winner is Mrs Grace Bilborough, 52 Cuthbert Street. In spite of his mates' teasing remarks Ted tries to keep calm while many questions and thoughts cross his mind. Why hadn't his colleagues in the office heard of this news? Of course they had been very busy the whole day. Why hadn't Grace rung him up? "But that was Grace all over" (**12**,5). However, she was a good wife and they had always looked after the family, paid their bills every week, and still put some money away. Ted is so absorbed in his thoughts that he hardly notices his mates' flattering him underneath their jokes. Letting them talk he looks out of the window, enjoying the beauty of the river and the banks in the evening sun. "There were two worlds, one looking towards the sunset with the dark land against it dreaming and still, and the other looking down stream over the silvery river to the other bank, on which all the light concentrated" (**13**,17ff.). Again and again the unexpected stroke of luck occupies his mind. £5000 – enough to make their old age secure. But how could Grace afford five and threepence for the lottery ticket? "His mind [darted] here and there suspiciously" (**14**,1f.). If she had been able to spend so much money on a ticket "he had been giving her too much for the housekeeping" (**14**,25f.). Leaving the ferry he walks home with his mates. The last to accompany him on his way home is Eric, who lives in a cottage at the end of the street. After Eric has opened his heart to Ted about his pressing financial problems, Ted promises his neighbour before they part: "I won't see you stuck, old man" (**15**,36). Then he enters the house, shouting expectantly: "Well, well, well, and where's my rich wife?" (**16**,17). However, Grace does not react at all but continues her work in the kitchen. After dinner, when the children have gone out to play and he is alone with his wife, Ted is unable to repress his curiosity any longer and embraces her, asking: "Gracie, aren't you pleased?" (**16**,29). Twitching away from him she says "yes" but goes into the kitchen where he follows her. Here he discovers that she has sold her mother's ring and chain in order to buy lottery tickets. Anticipating his question about what she is going to do with the money, she tells him: "I'm going away. By myself. Before it is too late. I'm going tomorrow. ... Beattie will come and look after you and the children" (**17**,13ff.). Shocked by her unexpected decision he asks: "Then you mean what it said in the paper, 'Last Hope'?" (**17**,20). And she answers, "Yes".

The setting of this story with its surprise ending is the Australian suburban lower middle class shortly after the Great Depression of the 1930s.[2] It is told by a third-person narrator who sees the events through the eyes of Ted Bilborough, a family man, whose idea of gender roles seems to be typical of most males of his time. To judge by their teasing remarks and suggestions Ted's mates obviously share his assumption that the husband has not only the privilege of disposing of the money he earns but also of his wife's money. A wife is merely given as much money as she needs for the housekeeping, just enough to make both ends meet. It is her task to do the housework and look after the children, a job that is considered to be of little importance, for Ted is convinced that "it was he who had had the hard time. All she had to do was stay at home and look after the house and the children. Nothing much in that" (**14**,16ff.). For Ted and his mates there is not the shadow of a doubt that their gender model is anything but natural and incontestable. Though Ted wonders why his wife is not "cheery and easy going", and notices that there is "something moody about her now" (**14**,14f.), it does not occur to him that she might be unhappy and dissatisfied with her role. Therefore, Grace's revelation of her secret actions and her emancipatory decision at the end of the story to use her own lottery money and go her own way strikes him like a bolt from the blue, although there are various hints in the story that their marriage is far from perfect.

---

[2] Cf. 'Emoh Ruo' (**16**,11): It was popular at that time in the history of Australian suburbia to give houses this kind of name (= Our Home, backwards) which has lower middle-class connotations.

# Teaching Unit I

## Preparation

The students should have read the story up to **15**,5 at home.
*Put the following quotes into context showing their significance for the story*:

- "Ted didn't know what to make of it." (**11**,4)
- " 'Keep the change, laddie', he said." (**11**,13)
- "But that was Grace all over." (**12**,5)
- "He wasn't interested in the news in the paper tonight." (**12**,33f.)
- "It gave his mind a stretched sort of feeling, just thinking of it." (**13**,28f.)
- "He hadn't noticed any difference in the housekeeping ..." (**13**,35)
- "... he'd been giving her too much for the housekeeping." (**14**,25f.)
- "It probably didn't mean a thing, just a lucky tag." (**14**,27f.)

## Setting, narrative technique and character

Working in groups, the students should scan the pages **11–15**,5 with regard to the following aspects. Afterwards the results can be summed up on the board:

1. the geographical, historical, and social setting
2. the narrative perspective and structural principle
3. the protagonist's character

**1. The setting**

The geographical setting of "The Lottery" is an Australian town situated on both sides of a river which can be crossed by a ferry. Upstream, in the western suburbs of the town (cf. sunset **13**,1f.) where the river bank rises steeply, there are "two churches and a broken frieze of pine trees" (**13**,8f.) and the wooded slopes are "scattered with houses"(**13**,11). The eastern part, dominated by "buildings serrating the sky", a "great silver gasometer" and "white oil tanks" (**13**,21ff.), is the industrial and commercial part of the town.

The historical setting of the story is the time shortly after the Great Depression (cf. **12**,14), i.e. the late 1930s or early 1940s. The events take place in the evening (cf. "6.15 p.m. ferry from town" **11**,5) of a warm workday shortly before sunset.

The social background is a lower middle-class family of four. Ted works as a clerk in an office while his wife, Grace, stays at home to "look after the house and the children" (**14**,17). They have been married for ten years. With the little money Ted earns the family can just make ends meet.

## 2. Narrative perspective

The story is told by an omniscient third-person narrator who is in control of the information, which contains not only the action but also the innermost thoughts of Ted Bilborough, the male protagonist. The assumption of omniscience makes it possible for the author not only to use a diversity of structural principles but also to delineate the protagonist's character.

*Structural principles*

The diversity of the author's structural principles is based on constant alternations between descriptive, dialogue and reflective parts, as the following diagram shows:

| page / line | parts | contents |
|---|---|---|
| (**11**,1–12) | *descriptive* | introduction to a crucial period in Ted's life |
| (**11**,13–20) | *dialogue* | information about his wife's winning the lottery |
| (**11**,21–**12**,5) | *descriptive* | Ted's reaction |
| (**12**,7–**12**,17) | *reflective* | Ted's stream of consciousness |
| (**12**,18–32) | *dialogue* | his mates' teasing and flattering |
| (**12**,33–**13**,24) | *descriptive* | the town seen from the river through Ted's eyes |
| (**13**,25–**14**,32) | *reflective* | Ted's stream of consciousness: "His mind darts here and there" (**14**,1f.). Reflections on the discrepancies in their married life. |
| (**14**,33–**15**,5) | *descriptive* | leaving the ferry |

## 3. The protagonist's character

According to the narrator's statements as well as Ted's image of himself (cf. **12**,7ff.), Ted Bilborough is a convivial companion, "always ready for a joke" (**12**,9), and liked by everybody. He is also a good citizen, husband and father. Since his marriage ten years ago he has always fulfilled his responsibilities towards the family. With the exception of a fortnight's holiday once a year, he has gone to work every day to support his family, has always paid his bills regularly and has even put some money away in spite of his low income. As a dutiful and thrifty man he is well informed about the housekeeping, and any irregularities arouse his suspicion and threaten his sense of security which is obviously not strongly developed. At the very beginning of the story, his mates' grins and the "little flutter of half derisive excitement all focused on himself" (**11**,8f.) when he steps onto the upper deck of the ferry, make him insecure. In order to cover up his diffidence he assumes "a hard boiled manner" (**11**,11f.). And when there is no longer any doubt about his wife's stroke of luck, he tries to hide his feelings beneath a cloak of nonchalance.

## Homework assignments

Re-read the pages **11–15**,5 and make notes on:
1. Ted's notion of gender roles
2. his state of mind
3. the atmosphere

# Teaching Unit II

## Conflict and atmosphere

### 1. A male-dominated society

*Which role does Ted assign to his wife?*

In Ted's view there are fixed male-female roles in married life. Whereas a wife's role is confined to the home where she has to "look after the house and the children" (**14**,17), a "good husband" has to bring "his money home" and is not allowed to look "at another woman" (**14**,10f.). And as both he and his wife fulfil these demands he is absolutely sure that "theirs was a model home" and that "everyone acknowledged it" (**14**,11f.). However, Ted is likewise convinced that there is "nothing much in" (**14**,17f.) his wife's household chores compared with the "hard time" (**14**,16) he has had. Regarding himself as a good husband and father who has devoted his life to his family, he is proud that his wife can "hold up her head" (**12**,11). But for Ted there is not the slightest doubt that as the family's provider he can decide how their money is spent, even that of his wife. Thus he is in control of every penny that is spent and even prides himself that he would notice "any difference in the housekeeping" (**13**,35). Consequently, after his wife's stroke of luck turns out to be true, all his thoughts revolve around the question of what he can do with the £5,000 she has won. In his opinion "he could do almost anything he could think of with five thousand pounds" (**13**,27f.).

*Is Ted's notion of a wife's role merely his personal conviction or do his mates share his opinion?*
All of Ted's mates obviously share his assumption that a husband can dispose of his wife's money. They take it for granted that Ted will use the £5,000 at his own discretion. As their teasing remarks make clear, they expect him to go "on a jag" (**12**,19), to go "off on a trip somewhere" (**12**,24), or to become "president of the Tennis Club" and generously "donate a silver cup" (**12**,25f.).

*What makes Ted suspicious that his position within the family might be in danger?*
Hardly has Ted become certain of his wife's winning £5,000 in prize money than he begins to feel doubtful about her sincerity. Why hadn't she let him know? "She could have rung up from Thompson's" (**12**,3). Yet this time he can find comfort in the thought that this is just her way. But in spite of all his efforts to get rid of his doubts he cannot help racking his brains about her odd behaviour, for "there was something secretive in Grace, and he'd thought she told him everything" (**14**,2f.). Where had the five and threepence for the lottery ticket come from? And why had she given it "that damnfool name 'Last Hope'?" (**14**,26f.). Though he has recently noticed that Grace is not "cheery and easy going" (**14**,14) it never occurs to him that she might be discontented with her existence as a mere housewife and mother. And therefore he dismisses 'Last Hope' from his mind as "just a lucky tag" (**14**,28).

**2. The atmosphere**
*Describe the prevailing atmosphere at the beginning of the story.*
On their way home from a hard day's work the men are relaxed and an atmosphere of serenity pervades the scene, finding its expression in the jocular conversation about Ted's wife's good luck. The men's cheerfulness is reinforced by the evening mood, the warmth of the setting sun like "a golden disc" (**13**,3), the quiet river and its banks seen from the ferry with their "slopes, wooded and scattered with houses" (**13**,10f.) on the western side of the river and the city skyline "showing up miraculously in that airy light" (**13**,24) on the eastern side.

*To what extent do the descriptions of the atmosphere and the scenery reflect Ted's present mood?*
Ted's state of mind is characterized by his being torn between great joy at Grace's unexpected luck and gnawing doubts about her sin-

cerity. This ambivalence is reflected in the evening mood and the scenery at sunset as seen through his eyes. There are two worlds in him like those he observes from the boat. On the one hand, "looking towards the sunset" there is "the dark land against it dreaming and still" (**13**,18f.) and, on the other hand, "looking down stream over the silvery river to the other bank" there are "the houses with windows of orange fire, [...], even a suggestion seen or imagined of red roofs, showing up miraculously in that airy light" (**13**,19ff.). Moreover, there are a great number of images and descriptions that reinforce Ted's ambivalent mood. While the boat vibrates "fussily" (**12**,35) the river is quiet. The bright sun "is sinking into a bank of grey cloud" (**13**,1f.), the river shows "thinly bright against the dark land" (**13**,11f.), the "smooth water" is "roughened by the turning tide, of frosty blue" (**13**,13f.) and the water gleams "silvery grey with dark clear scribblings upon it" (**13**,17).

### Homework

Read the story to the end.

## Teaching Unit III

### Dream and reality

*Describe Ted's state of mind when walking home with Eric and shortly before entering the house?*
During the conversation between Ted and his neighbour, Eric, it becomes evident that Ted's thoughts are still preoccupied with his wife's inscrutable behaviour, for his reactions to Eric's words are casual and naïve, showing that he is only half listening and does not realize what Eric is really up to (cf. diagram below). However, when he finally grasps what Eric's aim is, "a feeling of sweetness and happiness and power such as he had never expected to feel" (**15**,34f.) takes hold of him and for a time his misgivings disappear. Again, he has not the slightest doubt that it is up to him to decide what to do with his wife's money, and so he generously promises his neighbour, who is in dire straits, some financial support: "I won't see you stuck, old man" (**15**,36). This mood of elation continues after they have parted and Ted is standing in front of his house. Seeing that it is rather small and in need of repair "the revolutionary thought form[s] in his mind. 'We might leave here' " (**16**,8f.).

*Make a diagram showing Eric's tentative attempts to ask Ted for money and Ted's response.*

| Eric's strategy | | Ted's responses |
|---|---|---|
| I. <u>Trying to win Ted's favour</u> | | |
| "I'm awfully glad you've had this bit of luck" (**15**,11) (**a fawning approach**) | → | "I'm sure you are, Eric" (**15**,12) (**a casual answer**) |
| "There's nobody I'd sooner see have it" (**15**,13) (**a flattering remark**) | → | "That's very decent of you" (**15**,14) (**another casual answer**) |
| "I mean it" (**15**,15) (**confirmation**) | → | "Well, well, I wasn't looking for it" (**15**,16) (**a meaningless answer**) |
| II. <u>Coming to the point</u> | | |
| "We could do with a bit of luck like that in our house" (**15**,17) (**a first cautious attempt**) | → | "I bet you could" (**15**,18) (**a stupid answer**) |
| "There's an instalment on our house due next month. ... Nelly's got to come home ... Bob can't get anything to do" (**15**,19f.) (**describing his problems**) | → | "That's bad" (**15**,22) (**trivial answer**) |
| "She's expecting, so ... Mum and Dad will be let in for all that, too." (**15**,23f.) (**describing further problems**) | → | "It seems only the other day Nellie was a kid getting round on a scooter" (**15**,25f.) (**inappropriate answer**) |
| "They grow up, ... It's the instalment that's the rub. ... [Nellie] is our girl... " (**15**,27ff.) (**becoming more explicit**) | → | "You'll be as proud as a cow with two tails when you're a grandpa" (**15**,31) (**an exaggerated remark**) |
| "I suppose so." (**15**,32) (**giving up hope**) | → | At first there is **no reaction** but after the 'penny has dropped' he answers: **"I won't see you stuck,** old man" (**15**,36) |

## A surprise ending

### 1. Shattered dreams

*a) What are the different stages of Ted's disillusionment?*

First stage: Between hope and fear

Hardly has Ted entered the house when his elation, his day-dream of a secure future is gradually superseded by reality. As his assurance has gone and reluctance and shyness have taken hold of him, he hides his apprehension in the clumsy rhetorical question: "Well, well, well, and where's my rich wife?" (**16**,17). However, instead of a hearty welcome for her husband returning from a hard day's work, Grace immediately finds fault with him, saying in a tone of rejection: "You're late. ... The dinner is spoiling" (**16**,19). Her silence at the dinner table, which is only interrupted by her casual and more or less cryptic remark: "I got rid of the reporters" (**16**,21), leaves Ted in a mixture of misgiving and curiosity. He feels "himself, his voice, his stature dwindling" (**16**,23f.), and taking her awkwardly in his arms, he asks: "Gracie, aren't you pleased?" (**16**,29). Reluctantly she answers, "yes" after she has twisted out of his arms. She seems to be either embarrassed or fed up with him.

Second stage: Gaining certainty

Finally, she wills herself to tell the truth, and Ted not only gets to know where the money for the ticket came from, but he also finds out that she has probably been discontented with her life as wife and housewife for a long time and has spent her own money on the lottery tickets. Now, as she has the financial means to be independent of her husband, she takes a final, emancipatory step and goes her own way: "I'm going away. By myself. Before it is too late. I'm going tomorrow" (**17**,13f.). Her decision shatters both Ted's dreams of a happy future and his fixed image of married life, and of his own marriage in particular.

*b) What is the meaning of 'Last Hope'?*

Ted must make the bitter experience that this "damnfool name 'Last Hope'" was not "just a lucky tag" (**14**,26ff.) but that it had a concrete meaning. For his wife the term has two different meanings:

(I) As this ticket was the last chance before her "money was gone" (**17**,2) it was her last chance to make up for the money she has spent and lost on all the other lottery tickets.

(II) On the other hand, it was her last opportunity to win the money she needed to free herself from the dependence on her husband.

### 2. The overall meaning

The reader wonders why Grace used the name 'Last Hope Syndicate' (**11**,18f.). The word 'syndicate' usually stands for a group of people who have joined up to pursue a common interest. However, there is no indication that other people are involved. Therefore, it is possible that Grace saw herself as the mouthpiece of all those women who live under the same conditions and try to free themselves from an oppressive situation.

Thus the author could be said to show the dangers inherent in a traditional marriage with clear gender roles, where the partner who earns the money for both tends to dominate and the other one be subservient or secondary, because she / he is financially dependent, a fact that is / was bound to lead to conflict.

Nowadays it is believed that partnership can only be successful if both partners respect each other and are willing to acknowledge their partner's personal interests and needs. And, of course, nowadays it is possible and acceptable that both partners work.

**3. Discussion**

The following question is likely to trigger off a lively discussion:
*Is Ted a victim of circumstances or is his fate his own fault? Discuss.*

**4. Post-reading activities**

a) *The next day Ted meets his neighbour, Eric. Record their conversation in dialogue form.*

b) *Essay topics:*
- Write the first entry in Ted's diary after Grace has left him.
- On whose side are your sympathies? Give reasons for your opinion.
- Describe Ted's and Grace's married life from Grace's point of view.

Alan Marshall

# Trees Can Speak

## Interpretation and Teaching Notes

### Introductory Information

Although it is in no way justifiable to identify the narrator of a fictional work with the writer himself, there is hardly any doubt that in Marshall's works "the autobiographical element is predominant"[1]. Like many of his characters he constantly tried to overcome his disability which excluded him from taking part in the various activities of 'ordinary' people. However, his victory over his personal handicap may be symbolic of man's successful struggle against the adversities every human being is confronted with in his daily life. Yet, unlike many other people who share his fate, Marshall believed in the goodness of man, and nearly all his works reflect this conviction. Morever, Marshall's works display a genuine creed of 'mateship' (discussed on p.28f.) with the Aborigines, e.g. in "These Were My Tribesmen" (1965), a description of his visit to an Aboriginal reserve. A further distinctive feature of his writings is an intimate knowledge of the natural world and above all, of that of children. "Here", says Jack Lindsay, "we touch the unbroken lines of the communication he has kept with his own childhood and its fresh vivifying participation in the life of nature"[2]. "Trees can Speak" could be said to be archetypal of many of Marshall's stories with its disabled first-person narrator, its rural setting, and its simple narrative progression, which reaches its climax in a moment of revelation.

The first-person narrator, a young man disabled by infantile paralysis, meets 'Silent Joe', who he has been told never speaks. Driven by curiosity the narrator addresses him when he is washing gold on the banks of a creek. Joe only answers by the expression of his eyes or smiles. "He looked at me with kindliness and, for a moment, I saw the bush, not remote and pitying, but beckoning like a friend. He was akin to trees and they spoke through him" (**20**,6–8). The narrator

---

[1] Lindsay, Jack, "A Triumph over Adversity: Comments on Alan Marshall's Writing". *Meanjin* 28, no. 4, 1969, p. 437.

[2] ibid. p. 442.

follows Joe through the woods to a clearing where there is a mound of yellow clay around the edge of a shaft, which is spanned by a windlass with a bucket hanging from a roller. It is Joe's gold mine. Joe is pleased when the narrator is deeply impressed by the depth of it. At the narrator's request, Joe carefully lowers him down in a bucket to the dark bottom of the mine. Then he himself follows using a ladder. When he lights a candle at the bottom of the shaft the light reveals a tunnel branching out from the foot of the shaft. As the crippled narrator cannot move without crutches, Joe lifts him on to his back and together they reach the end of the tunnel, where Joe points at a "narrow reef which [forms] a diagonal scar across the rock" (**22**,32). Excited at the find of a speck of gold, the narrator asks many questions when they return to the foot of the shaft, which Joe answers "with eloquent expressions and shakes of the head" (**23**,4f.). When the candle flutters and finally dies, darkness covers the narrator like a blanket and he feels completely alone and cut off from life. When he is pulled up again into the dazzling sunlight he is more than happy to see the sky again: "I felt the solidity of earth beneath me. It was good to stand on something that didn't move, to feel sun on your face" (**23**,29ff.). Even when the narrator talks about himself and the people he has met, Joe listens with interest "drawing words from [him] as dry earth absorbs water" (**23**,36f.). The first and only word Joe pronounces is "Goodbye" (**24**,6) when the narrator leaves, and he comments: "it was as if a tree had spoken" (**24**,6).

There is hardly any doubt that Silent Joe, the hero of the story, represents an early phase of 'mateship', a term that has developed in the course of time and finally become a national ideal in Australia. In 1999 the Australian Prime Minister, John Howard, suggested a new section in the Constitution including 'mateship' as a cultural aspect of Australian identity[3]. "Mateship", says Bruce Kapferer, "is an egalitarian principle of natural sociality and reciprocity between equals"[4]. Indeed, Silent Joe's behaviour in "Trees Can Speak" is obviously determined by this principle of egalitarianism, for he regards the young man he happens to meet as an equal partner, whose physical disability he tries to compensate for with dedicated helpfulness. Moreover, Joe is first and foremost reminiscent of an earlier phase in the evolution of this Australian ideal, mateship as it was practised by the Australian 'bushman'. These pioneers worked in the

3 "... We value excellence as well as fairness, independence as dearly as mateship". From J. Howard's Draft *Preamble for the Australian Constitution*, quoted in: URL: www.womensconv.dynamite.com.au/smith.htm

4 Kapferer, B. *Legends of People, Myths of State: Violence, Intolerance and Political Culture in Sri Lanka and Australia.* Washington and London: Smithsonian Institution Press, 1988, p. 158.

outback, were isolated from other people, stayed together in small groups and showed a closer relationship to nature than the city dwellers. Therefore they regarded the Aboriginal, who lived in close touch with nature, as an ideal. Isolated from the rest of society the bushman had his own way of life and was considered as a non-communicative, silent and individualistic person who preferred to be out in natural surroundings. In contemporary literature he was romanticised as the representative of an idealistic Australian masculinity and of egalitarianism.

"... 'Tis hardship, drought and homelessness
That teach those Bushmen kindness:
The mateship born of barren lands,
Of toil and thirst and danger – ...
They tramp in mateship side by side –
The Protestant and "Roman" –
They call no biped lord or "sir",
And touch their hat to no man" [5]

He was the embodiment of Rousseau's image of the 'noble savage', symbolizing the innate goodness of man before he was exposed to the corrupting influences of civilization, and he established what Robert Burns calls in a different context "nature's social union"[6]. And in fact, Silent Joe has achieved this state of union for he has become part of nature. Thus, the narrator points out that "his eyes were grey, the greenish grey of the bush" (**19**,16f.), and that "he was akin to trees and they spoke through him" (**20**,7f.). Joe's non-verbal communication is another typical trait of the bushman. In Edward Dyson's "The Conquering Bush", Ned Darton, a bushman, marries a white townswoman and moves with his wife out to the bush. Though "he loved his wife, ... he neither talked, laughed, nor sang"[7]. Dyson makes clear that silence is not a specific trait of Ned's character, but a typical feature of the bushman: "Two bushmen will sit together by the fire for hours, smoking and mute, enjoying each other's society; 'in mute discourse' two bushmen will ride for twenty miles through the most desolate or the most fruitful region"[8].

---

[5] Lawson, Henry. *The Shearers.* (1901), quoted from URL: http://www.ozemail.com.au/~natinfo/lawson/the-shearers.htm – The poem is also included in: *A Collection of Australian Bush Verse*, ed. Allen, Gary, 1996.

[6] "... I'm truly sorry Man's dominion / Has broken Nature's social union, ..." Burns, R. "To a Mouse", in: *Collins Albatross Book of Verse*, Foreman, J. B., ed., London, 1960.

[7] Dyson, Edward. "The Conquering Bush", in: *The Penguin Book of 19th Century Australian Literature.* Ackland, Michael, ed. Penguin Books Australia, 1993, p. 72.

[8] ibid. p. 72.

# Teaching Unit I

## The opening: the encounter with 'Silent Joe'

**Preparation**
Read pages **19**,1 to **20**,13

**1. The setting**
*What do we get to know about the setting?*
The story is set in the Australian outback, on the pebbly bank of a creek (cf. **19**,13), where "the creek widen[s] into a pool" (**19**,9). The place is three miles away from the nearest town (cf. **19**,3f.).

**2. The opening technique**
*How does the narrator open the story?*
"Trees Can Speak" opens 'in medias res', plunging the reader into a crucial situation which is part of the related sequence of events. We can suppose that the narrator has been sitting in silence by the bank of the creek, when he suddenly hears "footsteps" (**19**,1). The supposition of initial silence is well founded and obvious, for the story opens with a noise (hearing) which is succeeded by a stranger's coming into view (sight).

**3. Narrative perspective**
*Preliminary considerations*
"Trees Can Speak" is written in the first-person. As the narrator's point of view is one of the most decisive factors for the character of a novel or short story, it is helpful for an interpretation to familiarize the students from the outset with the essential criteria that distinguish this point of view from other narrative perspectives. This task can be done in a class discussion. Then the results are summed up on the board, and finally presented by the teacher on a transparency in the form of a diagram.

*Universally valid features of the first-person narrator to be summed up on the board:*
a) It is a fictitious autobiography describing a crucial period in the narrator's life.
b) There is a time difference between the first-person narrator's telling or recording past events and the 'I' of the short story experiencing them.
c) Past events are presented as the narrator's own experiences.
d) They are seen from the narrator's perspective (= filter or lens) and judged by his or her subjective view of the world.

e) The narrator is inclined to push forward his or her own personality (egotism).
f) Unlike the omniscient narrator, he / she cannot slip into his fellow characters to describe their inner life.
g) Interior monologues and streams of consciousness are therefore limited to his or her own mind.

The following diagram may be presented on a transparency:

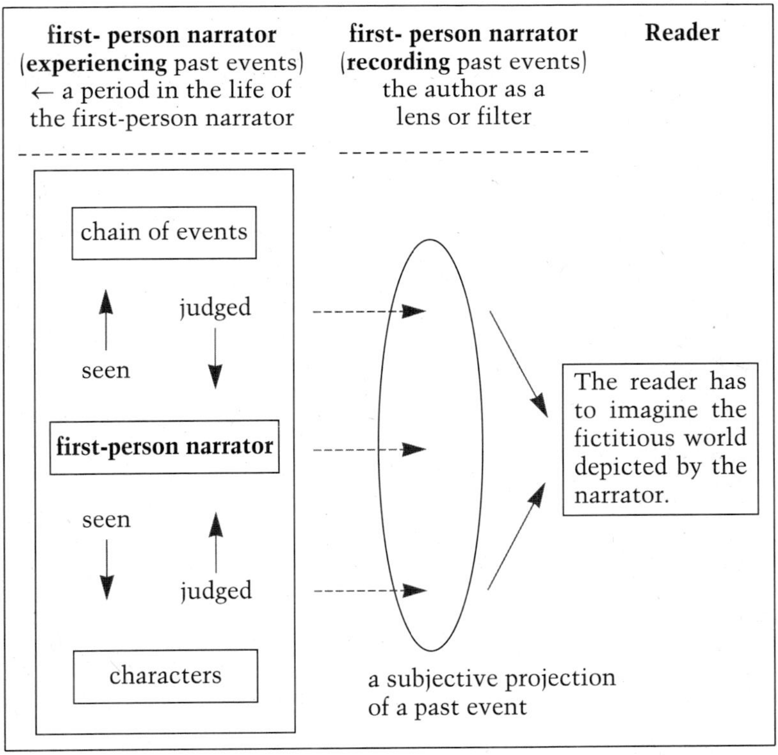


*What is the point of view in this story? Through whose eyes do we see things?*
The story is told by a first-person narrator, a young man who relates his encounter with Silent Joe. He is disabled ("I lifted my crutches" – **19**,13) and thus cut off from ordinary life. That is perhaps the reason why he seems to be an outsider who likes to withdraw from the company of people of the same age into the loneliness of nature. We hear that it was the store-keeper who had told him about Silent Joe (cf. **19** / 3ff.), and thus aroused the young narrator's curiosity.

*On page **21**,13 the narrator says: "Infantile paralysis ... It's a nuisance sometimes". What conclusion can you draw from this remark?*
In spite of his physical handicap the narrator tries to live a normal life; he does not really complain but only says that this disablement is "sometimes" a nuisance, not always.

**4. The structural principle**
*How does the author succeed in creating suspense and avoiding monotony? What structural principle does he use to this end?*
The following diagram will show that the dynamics and vitality of Marshall's short story are based on constant alternations between descriptive, reflective, and dialogue passages, while the descriptive parts often include judgements and comments.

| page / line | passages | contents |
|---|---|---|
| (**19**,1–2) | *descriptive* | audiovisual perception |
| (**19**,3–8) | *reflective* | remembering former conversation |
| (**19**,9–14) | *descriptive* | watching the stranger; personal reaction |
| (**19**,15) | *dialogue* | polite address |
| (**19**,16–18) | *descriptive and reflective* | reaction of the stranger; personal judgement |
| (**19**,19–20) | *descriptive* | the stranger's response |
| (**19**,21–27) | *descriptive* | watching the stranger closely |
| (**19**,28) | *dialogue* | question |
| (**19**,29–30) | *descriptive* | stranger's reaction to question |
| (**20**,1–2) | *dialogue* | narrator's question and comment, answered by the stranger's smile |
| (**20**,3–10) | *reflective* | reflection on the stranger's behaviour |
| (**20**,11–13) | *descriptive and reflective* | observation and comment |

**5. Personal response**

*Basing your view on the first 43 lines what impression does Silent Joe leave?*

*a) On the narrator*

Though the young man is curious to get to know the stranger, he is rather cautious when he encounters Silent Joe and remains "opposite him across the pool" (**19**,14). However, as soon as he recognizes that there is "no hostility in his look" (**19**,17) he moves nearer to him (cf. **19**,27). Finally, the expression in Joe's eyes and his smile (**20**,3) make him appear like a friend.

*b) On you, the reader. Do you like him or sympathize with him? Discuss!*

The students may choose suitable adjectives from the following list:

snobbish • amiable • gentle • courageous • upright • selfish • unselfish (altruistic) • impartial • bright-eyed • clever • reserved • witty • smart • intelligent • quick-witted • narrow-minded • stupid • naïve • foolish • pensive • sceptical • introspective • sensitive • sentimental • melancholic • timid • gloomy • ernest • morose • serene • calm • restless • uneasy • vivacious • impulsive • enthusiastic • touchy • reliable • stubborn • hypocritical • arrogant • fervent • energetic • happy • cheerful • passionate • envious • proud • sad • ruthless • sympathetic • pitiful • pitiless • emotional • stable • unstable • discontented • sincere • modest • thankful • humble • tolerant • honest • generous • friendly • hostile • patient • impatient • sociable • kind • polite • malicious • brutal • cruel • greedy • fair • unfair

## Homework

Read the story to the end and sum it up in the form of an entry in the narrator's diary.

# Teaching Unit II

## Homework check

Some students are asked to read their entries in the narrator's diary.

## Silent Joe, an individualist suggestive of an early Australian ideal: the bushman

*1. The Australian bushman was considered to be an individualistic person managing on his own and preferring to live in the freedom of nature. To what extent does Joe correspond to this image?*

Although the narrator leaves the reader in the dark about Joe's home, all the indications are that he does not live in the town, for there he is regarded as an inscrutable individual who never speaks but "makes himself understood by shaking or nodding his head" (**19**,5f.).

To all appearances he lives alone in the outback and enjoys his life independent of any external authority or pressure, relying on the scarce resources his natural environment provides him with and doing without any wealth and luxury. When the narrator says, pointing to some specks of gold: "Half the troubles of this world come from collections of specks like those" (**20**,1f.), he just smiles. Joe is an adventurer full of courage and enterprise, who defies the dangers of mining and is proud of his handiwork, "looking at it with a pleased expression" (**20**,29). The shaft of his mine is so deep that a stone pushed over the edge speeds "through a narrow darkness for a tense gap of time, then [rings] an ending from somewhere deep down in the earth" (**21**,1ff.), making the narrator exclaim: "Cripes, that's deep" (**21**,4). In conclusion one can say that Joe's lifestyle in many respects corresponds to that of the Australian pioneer, the bushman.

*2. Mateship, a principle practised by the bushman based on the idea that all people are equal, has become an Australian ideal. How does Joe put this principle into practice when he meets the disabled narrator?*

From the very beginning Silent Joe regards the disabled narrator as an equal partner. Seeing that there is "no hostility in [Joe's] look" (**19**,17) the narrator begins to have confidence in this stranger, asks questions, and tries to start a conversation. Joe's reactions are characterized by "kindliness" (**20**,6). When they walk side by side Joe studies "the track for [the cripple's] benefit" (**20**,15), removing limbs and branches. As soon as they reach the shaft of Joe's mine the narrator regrets not being able to climb down into the mine. However, Joe responds with "a sympathetic concern shading his face" (**21**,11f.) and even helps him to fulfil his wish by lowering him down the mine in a bucket. Finally, the harmony between them is so absolute that the young man can answer Joe's "unspoken intention as if it had been conveyed to [him] in words" (**22**,18f.). And Joe carries him on his back to the end of the tunnel that branches from the foot of the shaft. Here he lowers him "gently to the ground" (**22**,29f.). Having left the mine with Joe's help, the narrator tells him about himself and "the people [he] had met" (**23**,35). Joe listens "without moving" (**23**,36) and the narrator feels "the power of his interest drawing words from [him] as dry earth absorbs water" (**23**,36f.).

*3. Why does Joe dispense with verbal communication and how does his 'eloquent silence' work?*

From hearsay the young narrator knows that the man he has now met never speaks, though "he can talk if he wants to" (**19**,8). "He makes himself understood by shaking or nodding his head" (**19**,5f.), a trait which has earned him the nickname of 'Silent Joe'. Thus, it is quite understandable that he arouses the narrator's curiosity as soon as he turns up. And the first attempts to start a conversation with the stranger confirm that Joe indeed does not speak. However, the narrator soon learns that what people say and know about Joe is only half true, for he realizes that Joe makes himself understood not only by moving his head, but by his personal body language. Watching Joe's eyes, which are "grey, the greenish grey of the bush" (**19**,16f.), the narrator perceives that they speak "as plainly as if he had spoken" (**19**,19f.). Gradually it dawns on the narrator that this man has become part of nature, which does not use 'verbal' speech either. Thus Joe's smile moves over his face "as if wings had come and gone" (**20**,4f.) like those of an "egret in flight" (**20**,4), and the narrator intuitively senses that this man is "akin to trees" (**20**,8) and that "if [he] could only understand him [he] would understand the bush" (**20**,9f.). And even when Joe turns away "removed from contact by his silence" it is "not the silence of absent speech, but the eloquent silence of trees" (**20**,11ff.). Joe's non-verbal communication is so effective that the young narrator can answer his "unspoken intention as if it had been conveyed to [him] in words" (**22**,18f.). At the end when Joe's outstretched arm bridges "him to a box-tree that seemed strangely like himself" (**23**,32f.), "like a kindred tree" (**24**,4) and calls "Goodbye", it is "as if a tree had spoken" (**24**,6).

The teacher could quote the passage from Dyson's "The Conquering Bush" (cf. p. 27): "Two bushmen will sit together by the fire for hours, smoking and mute, enjoying each other's society; 'in mute discourse' two bushmen will ride for twenty miles through the most desolate or the most fruitful region". Thus he can give proof that 'mute discourse' or 'eloqent silence' is another characteristic of the Australian bushman.

## Nature as a partner

*1. What does the narrator learn from Joe?*
In the course of his encounter with Joe the narrator learns that man should regard himself as part of nature, and that nature is not our enemy, but a partner, a friend. Thus meeting Joe is to him like a discovery, a moment of revelation or 'epiphany'[1].

*2. By what stylistic features does the narrator make clear that nature is a partner? Scan the text again!*
The short story is full of personifications and similes which support the idea that nature is a partner and Joe a part of nature.

**Personification of nature and inanimate things:**

a) expressed by <u>verbs</u>:
"Trees can speak" (title) – "the sun pierced the canopy of branches" (**20**,18f.) – "Thin grass ... quivered" (**20**,22) – "the bush ... beckoning like a friend" (**20**,7) – "the light from the candle moved ahead of us, cleansing the tunnel of darkness" (**22**,27f.)

b) by an <u>adjective</u> (past participle):
"the tortured ladder" (**23**,14)

c) by a <u>noun</u>:
"the leaf mould breath of earth" (**20**,19f.) – "the mouth of the shaft" (**23**,26)

**Similes**:

a) referring to <u>conditions and distinctive features</u>:
Joe's eyes are grey like "the greenish grey of the bush" (**19**,17) – He is remote, removed from contact by his silence "like the gums" (**20**,11) – "the darkness had texture and weight like a blanket of black" (**23**,15f.) – "a grey box-tree ... seemed strangely like [Joe]" (**23**,32f.) – Joe is "standing against the grey box like a kindred tree" (**24**,4).

b) referring to <u>actions, proceedings</u>:
Joe's "powerful arms worked slowly like crank-shafts" (**21**,28) – the "candle shadows fluttered upon [Joe's] face like moths" (**22**,16f.) – a smile "moved over [Joe's] face ... as if wings had come and gone" (**20**,3ff.) – the narrator "suddenly began to rise like a bubble" (**23**,19f.) – "the power of [Joe's] interest drawing words from [the narrator] as dry earth absorbs water" (**23**,36f.).

---

[1] Cf. James Joyce, who used the word 'epiphany' in his verse and short experimental prose pieces to describe moments when the real truth about a person or object is revealed.

# Teaching Unit III

## Post-reading activities

*1. What else do you learn about the relationship between man, nature, and society in "Trees can Speak"?*

a) From Joe's behaviour:
- Man can be happy and content without riches, possessions and luxury.
- Verbal communication is not absolutely necessary for a harmonious coexistence between people (e.g. of different languages, ages or races).
- Solidarity, sympathy and charity are adequate means to overcome problems and difficulties.
- Goodness is an indispensable principle in our cynical age.
- People should respect their fellow-beings and regard them as equal partners (e.g. children, disabled people etc.).

b) From the narrator's behaviour:
- One should try to overcome the limiting factors in one's life (disability, poverty etc.) in order to achieve a broader view of life.
- Rumours and prejudices should not be relied on, but one should endeavour to find out the truth oneself.

*2. Write about a similar 'moment of revelation' you have had in your own life.*

John Morrison

# The Children

## Interpretation and Teaching Notes

### Introductory Information

The geographical setting of the story is the Dandenongs, mountain ranges which form part of the Eastern Highlands east of Melbourne, the capital of Victoria. The name comes from the Aboriginal word 'tanjenong' which means 'lofty'. Some hills are higher than 500 m. Because of the heavy rainfall and fertile soil the vegetation is luxuriant. Moreover, the Dandenong Ranges provide recreation as well as the water supply for the capital and there are three conservation areas: Sherbrooke Forest Park, Ferntree Gully and Churchill National Park.
Every year minor as well as serious bushfires blaze up in large areas of Australia, ravaging the country. These natural catastrophes are caused by great droughts and hot, stormy, northerly winds during the Australian summer. To reduce the extreme risk of fire the government has passed laws which prohibit making open fires on hot days. Even barbecues or lighting a match outdoors are forbidden on such days. Violations of these laws are punished with fines, but sometimes even with a term of imprisonment. As Morrison's short story "The Children" shows, these bushfires not only destroy the local flora and fauna, but also cause deaths among the local population. Not seldom do they lead to human tragedies and serious moral conflicts.

Shortly after a devastating bushfire in the Dandenongs, the first-person narrator, a reporter of the *Weekly*, wants to interview Mr Allen, a truck driver and carrier. When he arrives at his house, Mr Allen is about to leave his home "with all his worldly possessions" (**25**,3) on his truck. Both he and his truck are visibly marked by the serious effects of the fire. Expecting the intruder to be "another newshawk" (**25**,7), Mr Allen turns to the reporter "with frank hostility" (**25**,6). However, his unfriendliness changes a little as soon as he learns that the interviewer comes from the *Weekly* and not from one of the daily papers which "never tell a straight story" (**25**,12). Yet Mr Allen admits that "they did this time ... I'm not making excuses" (**25**,13). The fire has put a hard-working man in a moral dilemma with no real way out. While the fire was raging he saved his wife and his two children before he tried to rescue twenty school children and their teacher, a decision which has not only earned him the implacable hatred of their neighbours, but has also destroyed his self-respect. "I'll pay for it all the rest of my life. I'm that way now I can't bear the sight of my own kids" (**25**,18f.). Though he knows that any other man would have taken the same decision, he is harassed by a deep sense of guilt: "I should be shot – I wish to God they would shoot me! – but I'm still no worse than anybody else. I was the one it happened to, that's all. Them people who lost kids got a perfect right to hate my guts" (**27**,26–28). Only his wife's determination had held him back from risking his life and that of his whole family in a suicidal rescue bid: "I got into my head there was nothing else to do but cremate the lot, truck and everything in it. But the wife grabbed the wheel" (**28**,34–36).

As Morrison regards the nature of literature as a medium for commenting on ordinary people and their lives, the form of a story is only important as far as it is expedient to achieve this purpose. That is the reason why many of his stories are an amalgam of documentary and fiction. The same applies to his short story, "The Children", which is according to its form a fictional report of an interview between the first-person narrator, a reporter of a weekly paper, and a hard-working family man who has been trapped in an insoluble moral conflict. Both the narrator's role as an interviewer, whose position is outside the action, and the first-person perspective, which prevents him from entering his interviewee's mind and expressing his thoughts, warrant a maximum of objectivity. However, that does not stop the narrator from showing his sympathy, e.g. when he confesses: "I could think of nothing to say which wouldn't sound offensively platitudinous. It was the most unhappy assignment I had ever been given" (**26**,17–19), or at the end of the interview when he says: "I had an impulse to ask him what happened when he reached Burt's Creek, but restrained myself. His shame was painful to witness" (**29**,5–7). This obvious respect for Mr Allen's moral dilemma and his careful questioning during the interview give proof of the narrator's (and, we can presume, the author's) deep understanding of human weaknesses and his sympathy with the victim.

The basis of the reporter's interview is the question of Mr Allen's responsibility for the death of twenty school children and their teacher. Though he is convinced that "the Forestry Commission, the

---

[1] According to an e-mail from the Australian Bureau of Statistics [client.services@abs.gov.au] there is a place "Hunter" near Bendigo, Victoria, but not in the Dandenongs. The other places, Burt's Creek and Yileena, cannot be found "but it may be possible that the names are those of farming properties or fictional place names".

Education Department, and everybody in Burt's Creek and Yileena"[1] (**27**,2f.), are partly to blame for this catastrophe, he confirms that there is no doubt about his own responsibility: "But what's the use of talking? I was told to go and get the kids out, and I didn't do it. I got my own. Nothing else matters now" (**27**,15–17). But is he really guilty or did he become the victim of circumstances and his own human nature? These questions remain to be answered.

Whatever conclusion the reader may come to, Mr Allen is left with a deep sense of guilt which will haunt him for the rest of his life. And he feels, too, that he deserves the relentless hatred of his neighbours: "Them people who lost kids have got a perfect right to hate my guts" (**27**,28).

# Teaching Unit I

Read the first two pages (**25–26**,29)

## Setting and background

### 1. Geographical setting

As the story is set in the "Dandenongs" (**26**,26) the students (pairs or groups) could be asked to collect facts about this part of Australia from reference books, the internet or tourist offices.

### 2. Atmosphere and locale

*a) When you read the initial lines (25,1–6), what atmosphere do they convey? Do they fulfil the expectations the title evokes?*

Though the title "The Children" is a very general term leaving no room for any specific associations, the reader expects a story about children. However, he/she is surprised when the narrative starts with the introduction of a male adult ("He ...") who is about to leave his home for good. The description that follows conveys an atmosphere of devastation, desolation and hopelessness. The truck is "blackened and blistered" (**25**,2f.), the "dry old verandah" is "littered with dead leaves and odds and ends of rubbish" (**25**,4f.), and the owner's "bloodshot eyes" (**25**,5f.) give an inkling of overwork, stress, and exhaustion. Thus it dawns on the reader that an extraordinary event must have happened.

*b) To what extent are the initial lines a decisive factor for the following part of the story?*

The initial effect of desolation and hopelessness turns out to convey the basic mood of the story. By and by the reader learns that Mr Allen is tormented by a strong feeling of guilt: "I've got something to answer for all right, ... I'll pay for it all the rest of my life" (**25**,17f.), and a closer look at him gives an idea of what has happened. His boots are charred, his clothes covered with burned patches, his eyebrows singed and his face and hands blistered. And when the narrator's eye roves over the vicinity, the scale of the devastation becomes obvious. The sun in the sky is "a monstrous ball of copper glowing and fading behind the waves of smoke still drifting up from the valley" (**25**,29–30) and Mr Allen's house is "the first survivor after a tragic procession of stark chimney stacks and overturned water tanks" (**26**,3–5). Now the reader knows that a bushfire has ravaged the country.

*c) What is Mr Allen's social position before and after the bushfire?*
"Everybody's in on a fire" (**26**,28f.), says Mr Allen, and the reader is sure that this is no empty phrase, but a conviction that dominates his attitude towards society. His strong sense of duty becomes already apparent in the smallest social unit, his family. As a family man he has to support a family of four and his job is that of a "carrier" (**26**,28) – his truck is his living. And, indeed, Mr Allen is a hard-working man. His skilful and experienced handling of the tarpaulin of his truck is proof enough that he does his job regularly: "With the dexterity of a man who did it every day, he tied a sheepshank, ran the end of the rope through a ring under the decking, up through the eye of the knot, and back to the ring" (**25**,14ff.). Moreover, his way of life seems to have been rather unobtrusive, for he is only known to his neighbours. Thus the reporter, a man who usually knows everybody, had to ask "some men down the road ... to be directed to the Allen home" (**26**,20f.). It stands to reason that a man like Mr Allen is respected and liked by his fellow citizens. However, after the bushfire, this sympathy has obviously changed into the opposite, for the narrator reports that there was "hatred in the faces of some men down on the main road" (**26**,19f.) when he asked the way to Mr Allen's house. And Mr Allen, too, knows that he now deserves their hatred: "I've got something to answer for ... I'll pay for it all the rest of my life" (**25**,17f.).

*d) What does Mr Allen think about public opinion?*
Obviously, Mr Allen's experience with the printed press since the fire has been very negative, for as soon as he sees the interviewer approaching he reacts with "frank hostility" (**25**,6). He fears "another newshawk" (**25**,7). However, his hostile expression softens when he learns that the interviewer comes from the *Weekly*. "I've got nothing against the *Weekly*" (**25**,9f.), he says. He has clearly a higher opinion of the weekly paper than of the daily papers. Although the dailies "never tell a straight story" (**25**,12), as the first-person narrator remarks, Mr Allen admits that "they did this time" (**25**,13). Yet, in principle he does share the interviewer's critical opinion of the daily papers. But these papers influence the formation of public opinion and as they are often uncritical, they induce people to rush to false conclusions. Therefore, Mr Allen rightly complains that "people don't think enough, they don't think, that's all" (**25**,23).

# Teaching Unit II

## Reading assignment

The students should read the whole story and make notes on the following aspects:
1. narrative form and point of view
2. the interviewer's personal position
3. The reporter's interviewing technique
4. the chain of events

## The interviewer's role

### 1. Narrative form and point of view

*The author describes a crucial event in the life of Mr Allen. Which narrative form and perspective does he choose in order to do this?*
The events are told from a first-person narrator's perspective. As a reporter of a weekly paper he has been given the assignment to interview Mr Allen about the fire. However, the story is not confined to the recording of a mere alternation between questions and answers, but it also depicts the accompanying circumstances of the interview. Thus, according to its narrative form, the story is a fictional report of an interview.

*How does the author achieve a maximum of objectivity?*
On first thoughts, it seems to be contradictory that objectivity can be achieved by a first-person narrator. Yet the first-person narrator's perspective is one important way for the writer to be objective, for such a view-point permits him to forgo the assumption of omniscience, that means he is unable to enter the interviewee's mind and report his thinking. On the other hand, as a reporter and observer he is stationed on the fringe of the action following the course of events. Moreover, his sporadic descriptions, which give a realistic image of the scenery, contribute to objectivity, too. Thus, one can say that the first-person perspective, the narrator's position as a reporter, and his realistic descriptions ensure a maximum of objectivity.

### 2. The narrator's personal position

*Does the narrator's objectivity prevent him from disclosing where his sympathies lie?*
In spite of a maximum of objectivity the narrator betrays his understanding of Mr Allen's dilemma again and again. As Mr Allen's "shame [is] painful to witness" (**29**,6f.) the narrator admits that he "could think of nothing to say which wouldn't sound offensively platitudinous" (**26**,17f.), nor did he venture "to ask [Mr Allen] what happened when he reached Burt's Creek" (**29**,5f.). And shortly after

the beginning of the interview it dawns on him that this interview is "the most unhappy assignment [he] had ever been given" (**26**,18f.). When he describes the outward appearance of Mr Allen (cf. **25**,24ff.) as "a part of the great background of desolation" (**25**,25), the reader knows where the narrator's sympathies lie. And finally, his description of the Allen family's flight after the interview confirms his compassion for the victims: "Behind the dirty windscreen one could just discern the hunted faces of a man and a woman. Two children peeped out of a torn side-curtain" (**29**,19ff.) while people "watched with hard and bitter faces" (**29**,22).

**3. The reporter's interviewing technique**
The following assignment may be dealt with by partners or in groups.
*Scan the text and present the different stages of the narrator's method of interviewing in a diagram. Then sum up the characteristics of his procedure.*

| | |
|---|---|
| **1. Distinction between a daily paper and the *Weekly*** | "The *Weekly*, Mr Allen ... I've got nothing against the *Weekly*" (**25**,8f.)<br>"We know the dailies never tell a straight story" (**25**,12) |
| **2. Suggestion that the *Weekly* is factual and unprejudiced** | "We thought there might be something more to it" (**25**,11) |
| **3. Periods of respectful silence** | "I kept silent for a moment" (**25**,20)<br>"I just looked at him" (**27**,31)<br>"I waited, while he ..." (**28**,29) |
| **4. Showing understanding for Mr Allen's problem** | "We understand that, Mr Allen" (**25**,20) |
| **5. Achieving a response to a stimulus** | "I took out my cigarettes, and was pleased when he accepted one" (**26**,22) |
| **6. Expressing approval of Mr Allen's statements** | "I know" (**26**,9)<br>"Yes, I know" (**27**,33)<br>"No, you wouldn't read about it" (**29**,16) |
| **7. Close observation of what's happening around him** | "The door of the house opened. ... and large frightened eyes" (**26**,10ff.)<br>*continued on next page* |

| | |
|---|---|
| **8. Offering a cigarette to test Mr Allen's willingness to communicate** | "I took out my cigarettes, and was pleased when he accepted one. A man won't do that if he has decided not to talk to you" (**26**,22f.) |
| **9. Questions (or phrases) that are typical of an interviewer** | "How did it come to be you ?" (**26**,24)<br>"Vince picked you ..." (**26**,30)<br>"Then it isn't true ..." (**26**,33)<br>"You thought there was time to pick up ...?" (**27**,18f.)<br>"When did you first ...?" (**28**,18)<br>"You turned back ..." (**28**,37) |

**Conclusion:** In spite of Mr Allen's initial hostility towards the reporter, the interviewer succeeds in making his interviewee ready to talk by both tactical and emotional means. These are:
a) appealing to Mr Allen's power of judgement
b) making use of his journalistic experience
c) endeavouring to be objective and
d) showing respectful understanding, tact and sympathy for the victim.

## The chain of events and the question of guilt

### 1. The mere facts

The following diagram of the events related by Mr Allen should be drawn on the board:

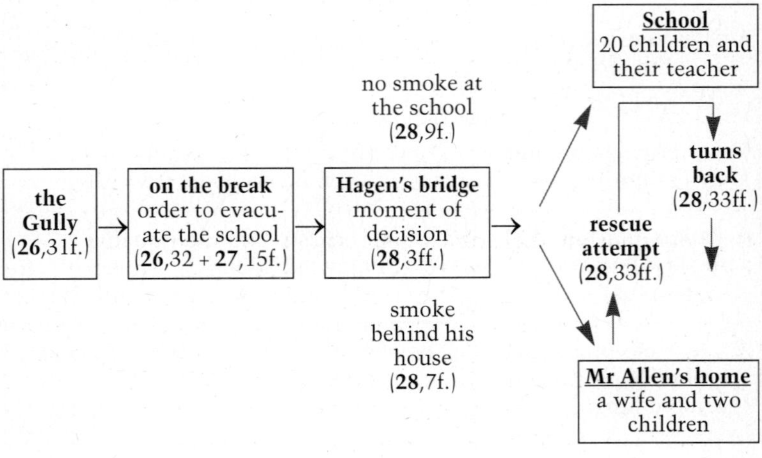

**2. The question of guilt**
This question is apt to trigger off a discussion:
*Is Mr Allen legally or morally guilty of the death of twenty children and their teacher?*
In order to stimulate the discussion the teacher should quote the following passage from the text.
Mr Allen: "there isn't another bloke in the world would have done anything else. I should be shot – I wish to God they would shoot me! – but I'm still no worse than anybody else" (**27**,25ff.).

Though it cannot be predicted what direction the discussion will take, the following aspects should be taken into account:

**Charges**:
a) responsible for the death of twenty children and their teacher
b) disregarded the order to save them
c) only saved his own family

**Evidence for the defence**:
- the Education Department should have sent the children home
- parents in Burt's Creek and Yileena should have kept them in their homes (**27**,4f.)
- the Forestry Commission was careless: there was "timber right up to the fence-lines!" (**27**,13f.)
- Mr Allen thought there was "time to pick up his own children first, and then go to the school" (**27**,18ff.)
- there was smoke at his own house, but none at the school (**28**,7ff.)
- the direction of the wind, his good truck and a good track from his home to the school assured him that he would be able to rescue the children later (cf. **28**,11f.)
- cut fern and blackberry nearby: "the school never had a hope" (**28**,23ff.)
- his wife "grabbed the wheel" (**28**,35f.) thus forcing him to turn back

## Homework

The following assignments should be prepared in groups:
**Group 1:** The interviewer distinguishes between 'dailies' and 'weeklies'. Make a diagram about the different types of newspaper, their distribution, their time of publication and their quality.
**Group 2:** Collect as many words as you can find connected with 'editorial staff' (e.g. publisher, etc.) and 'editorial contents' (e.g. article, etc.); or search for leading Australian newspapers on the internet: URL: (www.compucan.com/Newsstand/australian-newspapers.htm); and (www.nla.gov.au/oz/npapers.html).
**Group 3:** Is the press really free? Find points which limit the freedom of the press.

# Teaching Unit III

## Post-reading activity

The findings of each group are presented on the blackboard.

**Group 1:**

| The printed press | | | |
|---|---|---|---|
| **types** | **distribution** | **publication** | **quality** |
| **newspapers** | national<br>regional<br>local | dailies<br>(morning/<br>evening)<br>weeklies<br>Sunday papers | **quality press**<br>(having a more sophisticated reading public)<br>**tabloid press**<br>(sensational or yellow-press) |
| **periodicals**<br>magazines<br>reviews<br>journals<br>(professional ~<br>technical ~<br>trade~<br>financial ~) | national | weeklies<br>monthlies<br>quarterlies<br>semi-annuals<br>annuals | |

**Group 2:**

| Vocabulary |
|---|
| **editorial staff:** publisher • editor • editor-in-chief • reporter • photo reporter • cartoonist • correspondent • critic / reviewer • leader writer • contributor • free-lance journalist • advertising manager • 'agony aunt' • columnist • photographer |
| **editorial contents:** article • leader • ad(vertisement) • report • feuilleton • letter to the editor • news • local news • sports news • obituary • catchline • headline • caption • cartoon • agony column • gossip column • photos |

**Group 3:**

## The freedom of the press

The freedom of the press as freedom from political censorship is guaranteed in democratic countries, but there are still certain limits to freedom (as demonstrated in the diagram below):

**proprietor's interests**

1. political ambitions
2. financial interests
3. reduction of the price per copy (→ high circulation)

**advertiser's interests**

1. suppression of items or misplacing of stress [1] according to the interests of the advertisers
2. high circulation to help them to sell their goods

**reader's interests**

1. low price per copy
2. attractive and sensational items to please a large number of readers

---

[1] "There is no doubt that over whole tracts of social life, politics and economics we do not get information or interpretation from the Press. It is rather in the accumulation of small suppressions, a daily misplacing of stress than in any deliberate programme, that we find the influence of advertising." From *Voices of Civilization* by Denis Thompson.

Morris Lurie

# Pride and Joy

## Interpretation and Teaching Notes

### Introductory Information

The experiences Morris Lurie had during the years he lived and travelled abroad (1965–73) are reflected in his short story collection *Running Nicely*. That is why they cover an ample range of geographical places from Prague to the Great Barrier Reef, the latter being the setting of his story "Pride and Joy". The Great Barrier Reef extends for 2000 km off the northeastern coast of Australia and has an area of 208,000 square km, being the largest structure of coral reefs and islands in the world. Besides its scientific interest, the reef has become more and more popular with tourists. Meanwhile, it has been chosen as a World Heritage Area by the United Nations, and the Australian government has set up programmes to try to balance competing interests such as nature protection, tourism, shipping, and agriculture.

Like many of his short stories, "Pride and Joy" depicts characters with a clumsy love-hate for each other, misfits and perpetual tourists. With its swaggering, macho protagonist the story is largely a parody of Hemingway, the celebrated American author, for it is on this model and partly that of Clark Gable that its main character seems to base his public performances. However, though the story is superficially funny, the subject itself is not really funny at all, for it concentrates on a father-son relationship which is outwardly amusing but inwardly reveals distress and mental suffering.

One day the first-person narrator of "Pride and Joy", who is spending some time at a hotel on an island on the Great Barrier Reef in order to "sort out what [he] thought about a girl back home" (**33**,19), experiences the arrival of Ned Matthews, a boisterous, egoistic, and aggressively macho type who is used to giving orders and having them obeyed. The narrator himself, an introspective young man, forms a stark contrast to this phoney upstart, for he has very good manners, preferring to suffer sleepless nights with a snoring Irish roommate rather than cause bad feeling by changing his room. One morning Ned, the macho protagonist, who is "rich as blazes" (**34**,4f.) and owner of a luxury yacht, enters the breakfast room, followed by his son, Billy, a teenager of about 16 who walks "with an exaggerated swagger" (**31**,23f.), and Stan, a hired man in battered jeans and without shoes. They seem "like three ham actors playing at being tough" (**32**,15f.). After they have drained their glasses of beer in one gulp, the boy gives the pretty waitress a cocky smile and makes a ribald pass at her, while Ned orders four eggs each, some bacon, sausages, a lot of toast and black coffee. While they are waiting for their breakfast, Matthews coordinates their day's work. Later, at lunch they repeat their morning's performance. Again, Ned orders for all three and when his son is "cocky to the waitress" (**35**,8) he encourages him by commenting: "Keep at her, son" (**35**,9). In the evening they go to the bar where they gulp one alcoholic drink after another, with Billy trying to match his father drink for drink. "I can drink you under the table" says Billy and roaring with laughter Ned responds: "That'll be the day, son" (**36**,16ff.). But, we are told (**39**,8f.), Billy does in fact outdrink his father one night and has to help him to bed. Meanwhile, new tourists have arrived, among them a young woman of 22 or 23 with her mother. She has "dark hair to her shoulders, and looked like a princess" (**38**,30). Billy obviously takes a liking to the 'princess' and treats her very politely, while his father flashes his wealth and flatters both the girl and her mother. One night, the narrator returns to the hotel bar after hearing a huge commotion to find the 'princess' crying, her dress torn at the front, and Ned, bleary with drink, with his son shouting at him: "You're a pig! ... A dirty pig" (**41**,27). We can therefore surmise that Ned has torn the girl's dress. What follows is a wild brawl between father and son. Their repugnant behaviour towards the young woman makes the narrator realize how much he misses his girlfriend and longs for her: "I wanted my girl" (**41**,2). The following morning, at the breakfast table, Billy, for the first time, doesn't let his father boss him around and orders his own breakfast. He seems thus to be rejecting his father's example and deciding to go his own way.

As for the type of story, "Pride and Joy" is an 'initiation story'. Billy moves from being a follower of his father to his competitor, but after witnessing his father's physical violence against the 'princess' he withdraws his affection from him and makes his own decision, thus taking a major step towards manhood and independence. This 'initiation' motif has a long tradition in American literature from Mark Twain's *Huckleberry Finn*, and Hemingway's Nick Adams stories to Salinger's *The Catcher in the Rye*, to mention but a few. Mordecai Marcus distinguishes three stages of initiation according to the intensity and effect of the initiation[1]. According to this theory "Pride and Joy" obviously belongs to the first type of initation stories.

The events of the story are related by a first-person narrator, who turns out to be a reticent, introspective and considerate young man who observes his fellow guests closely and reflects upon them, thus forming a clear contrast to the loud-mouthed, arrogant and boorish protagonist who is accustomed to having his orders obeyed. Considering the narrator's loneliness, his taciturnity, and the vastness of the land – here the scattered islands of the Great Barrier Reef – one can rightly speak of a distinctively Australian story.

# Teaching Unit I

## Reading assignment

While reading pages **31** to **35**,2 the students (in pairs or groups) are asked to make notes on:
- the setting and atmosphere
- the opening technique.

Before analysing relevant aspects of these initial pages (**31**–**35**,2) it is a good idea to read this part aloud in class as if it were a play. This will help to display the characteristic tone of the story and intensify the experience of it.

---

[1] "An initiation story ... may or may not contain some form of ritual, but it should give some evidence that the change is at least likely to have permanent effects. ... Initiation stories obviously center on a variety of experiences and the initiations vary in effect. It will be useful, therefore, to divide initiations into types according to their power and effect. First, some initiations lead only to the threshold of maturity and understanding but do not definitely cross it. Such stories emphasize the shocking effect of experience, and their protagonists tend to be distinctly young. Second, some initiations take their protagonists across a threshold of maturity and understanding but leave them enmeshed in a struggle for certainty. These initiations sometimes involve self-discovery. Third, the most decisive initiations carry their protagonists firmly into maturity and understanding, or at least show them decisively embarked toward maturity. These initiations usually center on self-discovery." From Marcus, Mordecai. "What Is an Initiation Story?" in: *Critical Approaches to Fiction*. Shiv K. Kumar and Keith McKean, ed. New York, 1968, pp 203–204.

## 1. The setting

*Where is the story set?*

The setting is a tourist hotel on a beautiful, peaceful island on the Great Barrier Reef off the northeastern coast of Australia. This island is an ideal holiday place with its "buildings and huts scattered under" the green palm trees (**33**,11f.), which stand out well against the different tints of blue of the sky and the sea. With about "eighty people" (**33**,26) – mostly tourists – and "some goats" (**33**,22f.) the island is hardly populated and rather small, for walking around the island takes only "an hour and forty minutes" (**33**,13f.).

## 2. The atmosphere

*Describe the atmosphere before and after Ned Matthews' appearance.*

The peaceful atmosphere of the island and the unconcerned and unconstrained behaviour of the tourists is suddenly interrupted by the appearance of Mr Matthews, his son, Bill, and Stan, a hired man. As soon as they turn up the other guests stop talking and lapse into silence. And when the three newcomers walk "through the hushed dining-room" (**31**,29) only a few whispers can be heard. The interpersonal relations characterized by politeness and respect which have so far dominated the scene are disturbed by these boisterous and pompous fellows who behave like "three ham actors playing at being tough" (**32**,15f.). After Billy has made a vulgar pass at the waitress: "What's ya name, honey ? ... I always like to know the names of the girls I sleep with" (**32**,29f.), his father's "face [beams] with pride" (**32**,37). Then saying "Girl" to the waitress in a loud voice, Ned Matthews orders three breakfasts.

## 3. The opening technique

*How does the short story open and what is the purpose of this particular opening technique?*

"Pride and Joy" opens with a kind of prologue which traces the first-person narrator's first impression of Ned Matthews, the protagonist of the story. This opening technique serves the author's purpose in several ways. On the one hand, he plunges the reader into the atmosphere of Hemingway's world, a world of intense masculinity which found its expression both in the American writer's life and work. Walking "as though he'd just shot a lion, a mixture of offhand and proud" (**31**,7f.) and wrapping his fingers "around a large glass of frothy ice-cold beer" (**31**,12), Ned Matthews reminds the reader of Hemingway's special liking for big-game hunting and alcohol.

On the other hand, it offers the author the chance to provide the necessary background information concerning the protagonist's outward appearance by comparing him with Hemingway, whom the narrator has "never had the pleasure of meeting" (**31**,1), but knows from what he has read about him. Unlike his model, Ned has a moustache and not a "grizzly white beard"(**31**,5), is shorter and has less hair. However, "his chest was Hemingway, a broad barrel, stretching his shirt" (**31**,6f.).

### Homework

Working in groups, the students should do the following assignments:

**Group 1:** Collect facts about the Great Barrier Reef from reference books and the internet.

**Group 2:** Make notes on the typical characteristics of
a) a first-person narrator in general (cf. pp. 28–29) *and*
b) the first-person narrator in "Pride and Joy" (**31**–**35**,2)

**Group 3:** Make notes on the main characters (Ned and Billy).

# Teaching Unit II

## I. The Great Barrier Reef

One or two students from group 1 are asked to read out what they have found out about the Great Barrier Reef while the other students jot down notes.

## II. The narrative perspective

### Preliminary considerations

"Pride and Joy" is written in the first person. As the author's point of view is one of the most decisive factors for the character of a novel or short story, it is helpful for an interpretation to familiarize the students from the outset with the essential criteria that distinguish this point of view from other narrative perspectives. This task can be done in a class discussion. Then the results are summed up on the board, and finally presented by the teacher on a transparency in the form of a diagram.

**1. Universally valid characteristics of a first-person narrator summed up on the board.**

(For a general and detailed analysis of this perspective and diagrams see pp. 28–29.)

### 2. Specific characteristics of the first-person narrator in "Pride and Joy"

*What are the typical traits of the first-person narrator in "Pride and Joy"?*

At the very beginning of the story the first-person narrator's detailed description of Ned Matthews already provides proof that he is a close observer. And indeed, this assumption is confirmed in the course of events, which are disclosed through his critical eyes. He is an indecisive young man, who has withdrawn to this lonely island in order "to sort out what [he] thought about a girl back home. Did [he] want her? Did [he] want her forever?" (**33**,19ff.) Being an introspective and reticent person he does not reveal his thoughts or feelings to the other tourists, but prefers to retreat into the seclusion of the island by taking "a daily walk around the island, alone, just [he] and [his] thoughts" (**33**,20f.). As his behaviour is a model of polite restraint compared to that of the boisterous Ned Matthews, the reader soon feels that the author uses him as a clear contrast to the protagonist.

## III. The main characters

*Analyse the main characters:*

*1. Ned Matthews*

When Ned Matthews, his son, and the hired man make their first appearance they leave the impression of "three ham actors playing at being tough" (**32**,15f.). Ned Matthews, a millionaire who is "rich as blazes" (**34**,4f.), is a perpetual tourist sailing "around from island to island raising general hell" (**34**,8f.) on the *Southerly*, his beautiful yacht. He is a loud-mouthed upstart with no manners. He has no respect for other people, e.g. when he addresses the waitress as "girl" (**33**,2) or asks the narrator in a peremptory tone, "This free ?" (**32**,1) pointing at a vacant chair. Unlike the introspective and indecisive narrator, Ned is an attention-seeking macho, who is accustomed to "giving orders and ... having them obeyed" (**32**,4f.). He is a loutish and boisterous man, and when he enters the dining-room with his followers, a hush falls over the room while they make "a lot of noise with their chairs ... more noise than they had to" (**32**,5f.). The narrator feels that Ned is a phoney who bases his performances on well-known models like Hemingway and Clark Gable (cf. **35**,11).

*2. Billy Matthews*

At about 16 years of age Billy is a reflection of his father and his behaviour reminds the reader of the saying, 'like father like son'. Like Ned Matthews he walks "with an exaggerated swagger" holding "a glass of beer in his hand" (**31**,23f.) at 8 o'clock in the morning, "a Hemingway time for a glass of beer" (**31**,16). And regardless of the other people in the dining-room he bangs "his empty glass down on the table ... and then let[s] out a great burp" (**32**,11f.). Instead of reprimanding his son Ned encourages this ill-mannered behaviour by commenting: "Only way to start the day, son" (**32**,13f.). When the waitress comes to take their order Billy gives her "a cocky smile, his cigarette bobbing between his lips" (**32**,28). Without removing his cigarette from between his lips he bumptiously asks her, "What's ya name, honey ?" (**32**,29) and with his statement "I always like to know the names of the girls I sleep with" (**32**,29f.) his impertinence reaches its height.

## Homework

Extensive reading:
The students should re-read the pages **31–35**,2 and then try to read the remaining pages of the story without poring over too many details or looking up unknown words. They will then realize that they can already be confident in their own reading skills. Moreover, this method will extend and/or improve their guessing skills, i. e. guessing the meaning of unknown words from the context, from similarities with German or other foreign languages they know, and from words of the same word family. While reading they should make notes so as to enable them to give an oral summary in class.

# Teaching Unit III

## I. Checking the students' knowledge

a) One student gives an oral summary. Then the others are asked to add any facts or aspects that he / she has omitted.

b) *'Birds of a feather flock together'. Does this proverb turn out to be right in the story?*
Most tourists become silent when Ned gives his performances and like the narrator most of them are likely to avoid closer contact to him and his two companions. However, there are people who admire this show-off. Such a man is the fat stockbroker who is obviously impressed by Ned's macho behaviour, for he, too, is a self-important ass eager to attract attention. Thus, he wears "a lilac shirt and canary-yellow slacks and white shoes" (**35**,29f.) and having exposed himself too long to the sun he looks "scalded, like a lobster" (**35**,26f.). Ned Matthew's knowledge of alcoholic drinks impresses him so enormously that he can only keep "saying, 'Is that so?'" (**35**,28). He

is either stupid or a sponger who likes to drink at somebody else's expense.

*c) Which event confirms the first-person narrator's good manners?*
As the retired Irishman with whom the narrator shares his room snores "like an engine" (**36**,36) the narrator demands another room. He is asked to put up with his room for one more night as there is nothing free. But the following night there is not "a sound out of the Irishman all night" (**37**,11f.) and changing rooms now seems unnecessary. Although the following nights his roommate outdoes himself, "not only snoring but moaning, grunting, and giving whistles" (**37**,17f.) the narrator is eager not to "create bad feelings" (37,15) and prefers to suffer sleepless nights rather than make a fuss and change rooms.

## II. Defining the type of short story

### Preliminary consideration

In order to help the students to find out that "Pride and Joy" is an 'initiation story' the father-son relationship should be analysed more closely.

### The father-son relationship

*What is characteristic of the father-son relationship when the 'three ham actors' make their first appearance?*
Ned is proud of his son who seems to be his 'pride and joy' (cf. title). When Billy lets out a great burp Ned "smiles back, pleased with the performance" (**32**,13). Even when his son takes liberties with the waitress, Ned only says: "Easy, son" while "his face [is] beaming with pride" (**32**,36f.)

As Billy is willing to follow his father's example he seems to be either weak or stupid, for he readily obeys his orders, e.g. when Ned says: "Billy, you sit here" (**32**,3). Knowing that his father will order the breakfast, Billy leaves the menu on the table, and his objection: "Dad, I couldn't eat four eggs" (**33**,4) is completely disregarded by his father. However, in some respects Billy has already moved from follower to imitator, for he tries to behave like his father, smokes cigarettes and drinks beer at 8 o'clock in the morning. But his attempt to drain his glass in one gulp, as his father does, is only partly successful, because he has to "take a breath halfway down" (**32**,10).

By way of conclusion one can say that the relation between father and son is basically characterized by pride on the one hand and admiration for his father on the other hand.

*What are the further stages of development in the relationship between Billy and his father?*
Having been his father's follower and imitator at the beginning of the story, Billy in the end becomes his competitor. First at drinking, for

he "match[es] him drink for drink" (**36**,12) and even boasts that he "can drink [his father] under the table any day" (**36**,16f.). And indeed, we hear that one night he outdrinks him and has to carry him to bed (cf. **39**,8f.). Then one day, when a pretty young woman who looks "like a princess" (**38**,30), arrives with her mother at the hotel, Billy starts competing with his father for her attention. After dinner when Billy is politely talking to the girl, Ned appears like "a model of charm" (**39**,28) and hands a drink to both the mother and the girl. Later, at the steeplechase game, Mr Matthews pays for a round of champagne, staggers everybody "by shooting the bidding up to a hundred and fifty dollars" (**40**,20f.) and finally asks the princess "to move [his] horse for [him] in this race" (**40**,27). It seems that his ostentatious display of wealth and flattery have won the girl's favour.

The later events lie partly in obscurity, for the narrator goes outside. When he hears someone yelling "Help!" and the sound of breaking glass, he runs into the bar and sees the princess near the door. She is crying and holding the torn front of her dress "together with both hands" (**41**,23), while Billy and his father are facing each other, "their fists balled" (**41**,25). Billy is obviously disgusted with his father as he shouts: "You're a pig! ... A dirty pig! (**41**,27), and we must now assume that Ned has made a violent, sexual pass at the 'princess'. This incident helps Billy to take the first decisive step towards manhood and independence, for the next morning he opposes his father's orders, first by refusing the accustomed glass of beer in spite of his father's roaring: "Drink your beer" (**42**,12f.), and then by ordering his own breakfast.

Billy has thus experienced a phase of initiation into adulthood. Such stories are referred to as 'initiation stories' and have a long tradition in American literature from Mark Twain's *Huckleberry Finn*, and Hemingway's Nick Adams stories to Salinger's *The Catcher in the Rye*, to mention but a few.

# Teaching Unit IV

## Creative activities

After the incident in the bar Ned Matthews is accused of sexual harassment and damage to property. The first assignment may be done either by individual students, or in pairs / groups.

*1. Making a statement:*
Describe the events in the bar which lead to the brawl and its consequences from Billy's point of view. (This statement can serve as a basis for the following assignment.)

*2. Sitting in the hot seat:*
One student – a volunteer who is good at English – is asked to put himself in Ned's position. Before he is questioned by his fellow students he has to look for and collect arguments in his own defence for he will have to face criticism and justify his actions. In order to facilitate this didactic method and ensure its success, the other students should prepare some questions beforehand.

*3. Write the narrator's letter to his girlfriend after his experiences at the hotel.*

*4. Discussion:*
Morris Lurie once said about the distinctive atmosphere in his stories: "It's funny on the surface, but what I'm talking about is not really funny". Does this statement apply to "Pride and Joy"? Discuss.

Katharine Susannah Prichard

# Marlene

## Interpretation and Teaching Notes

### Introductory Information

No more boomerang
No more spear;
Now all civilized –
Colour bar and beer ...
One time naked,
Who never knew shame;
Now we put clothes on
To hide whatsaname

*Kath Walker 1964* [1]

"The mid-twenties saw a re-emergence of metropolitan Australian interest in the Aborigine. This stemmed from a number of incidents in the Centre and North-West. Two, in particular, were important. In June 1926, a party of police, in search of the murderers of a man called Hay in the Kimberleys [2], killed a number of Aborigines under suspicious circumstances and burned the bodies. This was the Umbali massacre. An outcry lead to the formation of a royal commission. When the results were published in 1927, the repercussions spread beyond Western Australia. [...] The debate in the press and in the federal parliament spread to the High Commission in London. The Aboriginal question was opening up for the federal government. [...] In June 1928 a prospector was murdered 256 kilometres north-west of Alice Springs on the Lander River. The reprisals have come down to history as the Coniston Killings. The crimes and action were old, but the debate which they generated in 1927–28 lasted into the thirties and was the most intense Australia had seen [...] This debate was the first concerted effort at national reflection on the respon-

---

[1] *The Oxford Book of Australian Women's Verse.* Susan Lever, ed. Melbourne: OUP, 1995, p. 105. Kath Walker (1920–93) is a renowned and very powerful Aboriginal poet and was the first to publish a collection of Aboriginal poems.

[2] Rough region in Western Australia between the Indian Ocean and the Great Sandy Desert where raw bush is broken only by unpredictable rivers, wonderful boulder-stacked cliffs, and small settlements.

sibilities of the Commonwealth toward the Aborigine. What is equally remarkable in the view of this late blooming interest is Katharine Prichard's discovery of the Ngarlawongga tribe[3] in 1926. It is unnecessary to assume much connection between these events and the kind of attention she brought to bear on the Aborigines. *Coonardoo*[4] shows us that [...] Katharine Prichard had, moved, with creative insight, into a new field of Australian experience. She did it in advance of any signalling from her society, and in defiance of its restrictive prejudice."[5]

Prichard's literary commitment to the indigenous Australians continued in the years following *Coonardo*. Her short story "Marlene", written in 1941, deals with the 'half-caste' theme, with those people who are alienated from both parent races. It is a reflection of the 'assimilation' era which recurred in Australian literature in the decades after the 1930s. In "Marlene" she criticizes the white men's treatment of Aborigines and half-castes in an indirect way, skilfully using the point of view of half-castes in order to blend past and present events, but the author's main motive is to draw attention to the abuse of Aboriginal and half-caste women by white men.

When Mrs Boyd, a stock farmer's wife, and Miss Cecily Allison, an English lady who wants to write a book about the Aborigines, visit the neighbouring half-caste camp on horseback, they find the camp in a most desolate condition. The primitive huts are no protection against the rain that has "been comin' down steady for two months" (**45**,14) and the hut dwellers' clothes are all soaked, grimy and threadbare. After more and more people have come out of the wurlies, Mrs Boyd asks them for Mollie, the sixteen-year-old half-caste girl who grew up with the Boyds and was now still useful to them "helping with the milking and feeding poddies" (**46**,5). But since the last Saturday night when Mr Edward drove her in to the pictures, the girl has not turned up on the farm. The crowd shifts uneasily, "eyes encounter[ed] and glance[d] aside" (**45**,24), for the question is obviously disturbing and has to be evaded. Instead of giving an answer the half-castes steer the conversation round to their own problems. And whenever the white woman returns to her question they use the same tactics. Thus they denounce the early settlers' rural expansion and their own expulsion and gradual dis-

---

[3] Aboriginal tribe in Western Australia

[4] Novel by K. S. Prichard which is regarded as the first important novel about the Aborigines and the first realistic description of the relationship between an Aboriginal woman and a white man.

[5] Healy J. J. *Literature and the Aborigine in Australia*. St Lucia: UQP, $1989^2$, p. 139f.

possession by brute force, as well as the removal of Aboriginal and half-caste children from their mothers in order to send them to mission stations to become 'good Australians'. Some of them use Mrs Boyd's visit as an opportunity to blame the white man for their present disastrous situation. Being uprooted, they live in primitive housing conditions, suffer from disease and have a low life expectancy. Many of them are unemployed or have badly-paid jobs and are treated "like dirt" (**48**,33). They have no rights and finally become addicted to alcohol or crime. Mrs Boyd's repeated attempts to inquire about Mollie remain unsuccessful. Only when she threatens "to let the Department know" (**51**,12) does the girl suddenly appear in the opening of a wurley with "a small bundle wrapped in a dirty shawl in her arms" (**51**,15f.). The girl has given birth to a baby named Marlene. "It's scandalous" (**51**,21), exclaims Mrs Boyd, "you ought to be ashamed of yourself" (**51**,27). Looking at the baby more closely Mrs Boyd recognizes that there is "something vaguely familiar in its tiny crumpled face" (**52**,11f.). Furiously she rides home, "curiously aged and grim" (**52**,20). On their way back Miss Allison suspects that the half-castes have "tried to spare the baby's grandmother, with simple kindness, knowing the truth behind Mollie's bravado" (**52**,31f.). Shortly after this incident the camp is moved on.

# Teaching Unit I

## Contents and opening technique

**Preparation:** The students are expected to have read the story to **49**,3.

**1. Comprehension questions (44–49,3)**
- Who is Miss Cecily Allison? (**44**,22ff.)
- How does Mrs Boyd behave towards the half-castes? (**45**,7)
- When did Mollie disappear? (**45**,33ff.)
- Why does Mrs Boyd ask for Mollie? (**46**,1–5)
- What happened to Wally Williams? (**46**,32ff.)
- How can Charley afford his liquor? (**47**,30)
- Why does Mrs Jackson refuse to go into the Old Women's Home? (**48**,28ff.)
- Where was she brought up? (**48**,21)
- What does she dream of? (**49**,1)

**2. The opening technique**
*How does the narrator open the story?*
Beginning with the description of the region and then gradually approaching the initial situation of the short story, the author uses the so-called 'zooming-in' technique, familiar to us from the cinema.

Leaving the woods, the third-person narrator gives us a wide view of the scenery: "crouched among rocks and wet undergrowth" (**44**,2) the camp is hardly visible and the township "in the valley below" is "lying under mist" (**44**,3). The existence of the camp is betrayed by "a breath of smoke" that hangs "in the air and [drifts] away among the trees" (**44**,6f.). The view then narrows to the two riders who are slowly approaching the camp detecting "the first humpy, then another and another" (**44**,8f.) and finally arriving at "a rough open space" (**44**,10), the centre of the camp, where the fierce barking of the dogs announces the newcomers.

**3. Phase of preparation (49,3 – end)**
First the students are asked to read the last pages of the story silently so as to understand the details. Then they should be read together in class. In order to intensify the dramatic effect of this part of the story it should be read in parts like a playreading.

**4. Reading check**
*Put the following quotes into context and show their significance for the story.*
- "You're the granddaughter of one of the early settlers" (**49**,10)
- "All we're allowed to do is draw rations and rot" (**49**,23)
- "I've always given you work on my farm when I could" (**49**,29)
- "Do the aboriginals treat half-castes better ? " (**50**,8)
- "... the Protector won't let Penny Carnarvon marry him" (**50**,28f.)
- "But I'll have to let the Department know" (**51**,12)
- "But you're only a child. ... You're not sixteen" (**51**,19)
- "... there was something vaguely familiar in its tiny crumpled face" (**52**,11f.)
- "... the older woman sagged in her saddle, curiously aged and grim" (**52**,20)

**Homework:** Re-read the story and make notes on:
- the narrative perspective
- the narrative technique
- the characters (minor and major characters)
- the fate of the Aboriginal people.

This assignment can be done in pairs or groups.

# Teaching Unit II

## Form and style

**I. The narrative perspective**
*What point of view dominates in the story?*

The story is basically written from the point of view of a third-person, observer-narrator who restricts himself mainly to the description of what the characters do or say. This 'camera eye' technique is a logical continuation of the initial 'zooming-in' technique. However, there are two short moments when the narrator refers to Mrs Boyd's thoughts: "Mrs Boyd guessed [...] with her own kind" (**46**,12–14) and "Mrs Boyd inquired, willing to humour them" (**46**,27f.). In the last lines beginning with "She wondered whether ..." (**52**,25ff.), we can even listen to Miss Allison's interior monologue. Thus one may speak in this case of 'selective or partial omniscience'.

**II. The narrative technique**

*How does the narrator succeed in increasing suspense?*

Though the short story is lacking in action and is mainly based on a dialogue between socially and economically unequal partners – a white landowner and poor half-castes – the author succeds in maintaining and even increasing suspense by using a specific principle. It is the 'leitmotif-like' repetition of Mrs Boyd's query about Mollie. Her first question: "Where's Mollie?" (**44**,15) escapes notice because of the flurry of excitement caused by the sudden and unexpected arrival of Mrs Boyd and her lady companion. But each time she repeats her question, the half-castes react strangely and are eager to change the subject, thus increasing the reader's curiosity. Finally, Mrs Boyd threatens to inform the Department. In order to escape this impending danger, Mollie emerges at last from one of the wurlies.

| **Mrs Boyd's attempts** | **the half-castes' reactions** | **the reader's reactions** |
|---|---|---|
| 1. "Where's Mollie?" (**44**,15) | no answer | indifference<br>↓ |
| 2. "Where is she?" (**45**,22f.)<br>"Where is Mollie?" (**45**,33) | "The crowd shifted uneasily. Eyes encountered and glanced aside" (**45**,24)<br>→ conversation about Mollie's character | interest<br>↓ |
| 3. "But where is she?" (**46**,7) | "The crowd surged. Obviously the question was disturbing: it had to be evaded" (**46**,8f.)<br>→ Bill Bibblemun's death and other subjects | curiosity |

| | | |
|---|---|---|
| 4. "… have you made up your minds yet to tell me about Mollie?" (**48**,4f.) | "The faces about her changed. There was a moment of sombre, unresponsive silence" (**48**,6f.) → Mrs Jackson's fate and that of her people | ↓ curiosity and suspense |
| 5. "But where's Mollie?" (**51**,6)<br><br>Threat: "I'll have to let the Department know –" (**51**,12) | "There was a disconcerted shuffling and searching for something to say." (**51**,7f.)<br><br>Mollie appears "in the opening of a wurley" (**51**,13f.) | ↓<br>climax of curiosity and suspense |

## III. The characters

### 1. Minor characters

*Who are the minor characters and what is their significance?*

First, there are some unnamed women who merely serve as links in the course of the discussion, whereas others, e.g. Tilly (cf. **44**,29f.) and Mrs Jackson (cf. **50**,24f.), interfere soothingly or defend other half-castes against calumny. The latter is true of Tilly who speaks up for Wally Williams (cf. **46**,34ff.). Then there is Mrs Jackson who serves as an example of the desolate situation of the older half-castes (cf. **48**,8–**49**,3), and Ruby who tells of the state of health at the camp (cf. **46**,26). Some men, too, provide short background information, e.g. George on Wally Williams (cf. **46**,32). Finally, four characters are only mentioned by name in order to exemplify typical aspects of the half-castes' fate. Thus, Bill Bibblemun's death draws the reader's attention to the black people's delicate health and and low life expectancy (cf. **46**,15ff.), Wally William's imprisonment to unemployment and criminality (cf. **46**,33ff.), Charley's miserable condition to alcoholism (cf. **47**,24ff.) and Penny Carnarvon's problem to the Aborigines' lack of rights (cf. **50**,28ff.).

### 2. Major characters

*Outline Mrs Boyd's character.*

Mrs Boyd is a woman "capable of managing her own affairs" (**45**,6), and her appearance at the beginning of the story seems to confirm the narrator's statement that she is "authoritative, but kind and friendly" (**45**,7). However, it soon dawns on the reader that her kindness and friendliness are rather limited and superficial. After expressing her indignation about the degrading living conditions at the camp (cf. **45**,21) she abruptly returns to her own interests instead of going deeper into the problem: "But what I came about […] is

Mollie" (**45**,22). And whenever someone does not come up to her own moral principles she becomes reproachful, furious, and mean, e.g. when she chides Mollie for the birth of her illegitimate child: "It's scandalous (**51**,21) [...] You ought to be ashamed of yourself" (**51**,27). Her authoritative bearing, too, is questionable, for each time her personal authority is called for, she entrenches herself behind the government authorities. When Albert blatantly accuses her and white people in general she uses what are often called female tactics. First she promises help: "I'll see what I can do about it" (**49**,8) so as to soothe him, then she shows understanding for his biting criticism and promises improvement: "Something will have to be done about it" (**49**,18), but soon she has to defend herself: "You can't say I haven't tried to help you" (**49**,28). In the end, finding herself cornered, she tries to intimidate him by threatening him with the authorities. "If you're not careful you'll find yourself being moved on" (**49**,35f.), a threat that is finally carried out (cf. **52**,34f.).

*What role does Miss Allison play and what are her typical character traits?*

As a young woman from England who is "going to write a book about the aborigines" (**44**,23f.) Miss Cecily Allison is an objective and impartial observer. Therefore she remains passive throughout the conversation between Mrs Boyd and the half-castes, probably following every word intently and absorbing all the information as she is new to this environment. Only once does she join in when she asks for additional information, i.e. about the relationship between Aboriginals and half-castes (cf. **50**,8f. and **50**,16), indirectly criticising Albert for his outburst against the whites. But she abstains from giving her personal opinion. However, when she sees the baby we learn more about her feelings and thoughts, although her first reaction is "mechanical" (**52**,14). Unlike Mrs Boyd she seems to sympathize with Mollie or at least shows an interest by asking her: "What are you going to call her?" (**52**,14f.).

Here then the reader feels that, contrary to Mrs Boyd's patronizing attitude, this young woman seems to realize that the half-castes have a right to aspire to "the ways and ideas of the white race" (**52**,28f.). She has, of course, not been involved herself in Australia's crimes against humanity. She acts as a corrective to Mrs Boyd's mean and hypocritical behaviour when she reacts to her self-righteous judgement that these half-castes are "an immoral lot" (**52**,22) with the question: "What about the whites who are responsible for them?" (**52**,23). In the interior monologue that follows she comments on and interprets the scene she has just witnessed, reflecting on the white man's responsibility and interpreting the half-castes' behaviour towards Mrs Boyd as an attempt "to spare the baby's grandmother" (**52**,31), for she has probably noticed that the baby looks like Mr Edward.

*What is your attitude towards Mollie? Is she immoral and irresponsible, to be pitied, or perhaps to be envied? Discuss.*

**Homework:** Find an appropriate heading for Albert's verbal attack (**49**,4–**50**,27) and then transform this passage into a stage-script.

# Teaching Unit III

## Confrontation and conflict

**Homework check:**

1. After the students have made their suggestions, the best heading is recorded on the blackboard.
2. One or two stage-scripts are acted out in class and commented on.

**1. A blatant accusation of the white man's ruthlessness (49,4–50,27).**
*How and why does Albert differ from the other half-castes?*
The naive-sounding Ruby tells us in a tone of both admiration and apology that Albert is "real clever: he can read and write as good as any white man" and that "when he went to school he could beat any of the boys" (**50**,2f.). And indeed, Albert is the only half-caste at the camp who stands up to Mrs Boyd, this capable and authoritative woman. His first words at the beginning of the short story display a critical character who dares to criticize Mrs Boyd's early visit (cf. **44**,27f.). And when old Mrs Jackson's miserable situation is being discussed, his anger erupts. For him the basic cause of the black people's wretchedness is the white men's greed and egoism, for "the whites grab all they can for themselves", as well as their lack of compassion, for they "let even their own relatives starve" (**50**,6f.), meaning the half-castes. Thus the white settlers had once killed off the black Australians, dispossessed them of their legitimate land, and uprooted them. When Mrs Boyd promises to "see what [she] can do" (**49**,8) about Myrtle's accomodation which is unfit for a human being, he cynically refers to the paradox that Mrs Jackson, the granddaughter of the original, legitimate owner of the land, is offered help by Mrs Boyd, the granddaughter of an illegitimate owner of the land.

In a sarcastic and reproachful tone he attacks the white men's ruthlessness, for these usurpers have deprived their black fellow-beings of their rights and have degraded them to a race of beggars who are allowed to "draw rations and rot" (**49**,23). It stands to reason that such a rebel and "crazy agitator" (**49**,34) like Albert is a menace to the peaceful and wealthy life of the whites and so Mrs. Boyd threatens him with expulsion from the district. However the 'rebel' does not let himself be intimidated, but responds with a malicious grin: "I'll rememberr you said so, Mrs Boyd" (**49**,37).

**2. An unbroken sequence of crimes against human rights and humanity**
*How does the narrator succeed in giving a complete picture of the situation of the black people and the half-castes?*
The information the reader is provided with is either based on the observations made by the narrator or on the comments made by the half-castes while they are trying to evade Mrs Boyd's query about Mollie. Thus the author blends past events, which are mainly referred to by Albert, and the present situation (1941) of the blacks and the half-castes, which is characterized by a large spectrum of crimes against human rights. These can be summed up in a table.

**Past events**

Murder and dispossession of the Aborigines (**49**,10ff.)
Separation of children from their mothers to be educated at a mission (cf. **48**,21)

**Consequences for the present (1941)**

- numbers of half-castes as a result of the abuse of black women by white men (cf. **45**,28ff.)
- alienation from both parent races (cf. **50**,10ff.)
- unemployment (cf. **47**,10; **49**,20ff.) or badly-paid jobs (cf. **49**,30f.)
- primitive living conditions and accomodation unfit for human beings (cf. **44**,3f.; **44**,17ff.; **45**,19; **45**,25ff.)
- susceptibility to diseases partly imported by the white men:
  1. pneumonia (cf. **46**,15) • 2. rheumatism (cf. **48**,9) • 3. measles (cf. **46**,26)
- high mortality rate and low life expectancy
- alcoholism (cf. **47**,25ff.)
- criminality (cf. **46**,33ff.)
- lack of rights (cf. **49**,19ff. + **50**,28ff.)
- lack of respect shown by whites (cf. **48**,32f.)
- danger of losing their self-esteem (cf. **48**,33ff.)

**3. The ending**
*Why is Mrs Boyd "curiously aged and grim" (**52**,20) after her visit to the camp?*
This question is likely to trigger off a lively discussion.

**Homework or post-reading activities:**
1. Write an essay about Mrs Boyd's return home.
2. Write the first entry in Mrs Boyd's diary after her experiences at the camp.

Archie Weller

# Pension Day

## Interpretation and Teaching Notes

### Introductory Information

If you want me, walk along a street
Holding in each dark doorway,
Nothing, but your middle-class do-gooder fear;
Then stop, look down, right down –
An empty bottle, a sprawled black body,
Pink streaming urine stinking of your wine. [...]
If you want me, try your grassless parks,
In solitude, old men drinking life away.

*Colin Johnson 1986*[1]

When the Australian Aborigines encountered the first white men, they regarded them as mythic beings or spirits of the dead. This erroneous idea, however, was soon disproved by reality. But even when Captain Arthur Phillip established the first convict settlement at Sydney in 1788, they called him 'Be-anga', meaning 'father', because he treated them respectfully. Yet Phillip failed to establish peace between the settlers and the Aboriginals, for as soon as he had returned to England in 1792 the massacre of the native population began. On July 20th, 1816, Governor Lachlan Macquarie enacted his 'Proclamation of Native Outlawry' which authorized any white man to kill any Aborigine without being punished. This was the starting signal for 'Abo-Hunting' in all parts of the Australian continent. During the so-called period of 'pacification by force' lasting up to 1880, the Aboriginal population, which was about 300,000 in 1788, was reduced to ca. 120,000. Those who were not killed by the whites succumbed to imported diseases. The survivors fled into the bush or remained and submitted to the influence of missions or they sought refuge in camps or sheep and cattle stations where they were exploited as cheap labour. In the course of time most of them learned

[1] from: *The Song-Circle of Jacky and Selected Poems*. Melbourne: Hyland House, 1986, p. 35–36. Mudrooroo Narogin (Colin Johnson) is a member of the Aboriginal Arts Unit committee of the Australia Council.

that their only alternative was to adapt to the white man's way of life although this led to the pauperization of the Aboriginal peoples.

The present population of native Australians is estimated at about 360,000 and only one third of them are of homogeneous ancestry, whereas the rest are mixed Aboriginal and European. The majority of the full bloods live in the North of Queensland and Western Australia. Here some still live in tribes, but only a minority continue the nomadic hunting life of their ancestors. Today most of them live in Aboriginal communities, government reserves or former mission stations, depending mainly on social security or earning a little money as casual workers. Many of these uprooted human beings are addicted to alcohol although some of them have tried to assimilate into the white man's urban way of life.

In large areas of southern and mid-eastern Australia Aborigines of mixed Aboriginal and European parentage have given up their traditional life, while those native Australians who live in fringe settlements are trying to integrate European aspects into their culture.[2]

**Dreaming or Dreamtime**[3]

*"... he had recounted his stories to his young woman way up in the red, swirling Dreaming."* (**57**,18ff.)

The encounter between the white settlers and the Aborigines not only meant a confrontation between two different races and cultures but also the clash of two contrasting world views. Whereas the Christian settlers misinterpreted their God's advice to "replenish the earth, and subdue it"[4] as a challenge to exploit nature, the traditional Aboriginals regarded human beings as a part of nature, intimately linked with the animal species and even with mythic beings. Their conviction was based on the Dreamtime, a mythological period of time with a beginning but no foreseeable end. It was the creative period when mythic, ancestral beings shaped the environment, established human life and fashioned the law. The Dreaming includes totemism, the belief in the relationship between social groups, individuals and animals or other natural things. The link between the people and their ancestral beings are totems, who reveal themselves in the Dreamtime and provide man with an imperishable identity starting at the beginning of time and continuing into the future.

---

[2] For further information see: Berndt, R. M. & Berndt, C. H., *The World of the First Australians. Aboriginal Tradition Life: Past and Present*. London: Angus & Robertson, 1964. And Elkin, A. P. *The Australian Aborigines*. Sydney: Angus & Robertson, 1979.

[3] For further information see: Lawlor, Robert. *Voices of the First Day: Awakening in the Aboriginal Dreamtime, Inner Traditions*. 1991.

[4] *Genesis*, I, 28.

**Blood feud**

*"A life for a life. That was how the law had worked since before everything. The law was the law."* (**55**,1f)

The old full-blood Aborigine in Weller's "Pension Day" had obviously revenged the murder of a close relative when he was about 18 years old, and then the white men had arrested him. An imprisonment of seven years had followed "for a crime he could not understand" (**54**,25f.). However, to uphold the accepted codes of his people adequate sanctions had been natural and lawful, and so killing had required counterkilling.

Among the Australian Aborigines compensation in the form of regulated fighting was frequently used as a substitute for blood feud when dissension arose between two kinship groups. To protect their individual members against physical harm or defamatory actions by outsiders, there was a strong collective solidarity within each group which meant that the offender's kinsmen were also held collectively responsible for the misdeeds of each of their members.

In Archie Weller's "Pension Day" an old, homeless Wongi Aborigine, whose worn clothes show that he is impoverished, is sitting in a park trying to seek comfort in alcohol. He has lost his past, his people and his rural homeland, for when he was about 18 years old he had revenged the murder of one of his people as the laws of his society had required. "A life for a life. That was how the law had worked since before everything" (**55**,1f.). However, the white police – he had seldom seen a white man before – had arrested him before the eyes of his people ,"torn him away from his red land's breast for a crime he could not understand" (**54**,25f.), and taken him to jail. After spending seven years in prison he was still young and strong but he knew that he would never be able to go home, for either the relatives of his victim or the new husband of his wife would kill him. "So he had no country. He had no home" (**56**,1).

With little knowledge of English he had a lot of trouble to find employment. But a good white boss had given him work and "found him a good half-caste girl from the nearby mission" (**56**,9f.), who had taught him a little more English. They had been happy in their house with their three children. When the fourth child was born his wife had died. In his desolation and loneliness he started drinking. After starting a brawl amongst the Nyoongah people he was put in prison again where his boss had got him out the next morning. "He followed his boss's footsteps like a huge dog. So he lost even his pride and gave up" (**58**,10ff.). Then, having been uprooted a second time. he had retreated from his fellow-beings, living "in a little humpy in the bush" (**58**,14f.), where no one could find him. His children had been taken away from him by the Community Welfare and he never saw them again.

Now, on pension day, he is sitting in the park, sneered at by the people, while Aboriginal boys even steal $20 from him. Though he had been known and admired for his strength and power when he was young, he is unable to hold his own against them. After everyone has left the park and gone home there is a thunderstorm. But the old man has no other shelter but an old tree where he empties his bottle of methylated spirits. "He suddenly vomits up all his pension day money. All over his coat and face and trousers" (**60**,19f.). He falls asleep. "The old Aboriginal lies underneath his tree that cannot help him, for it, too, is old and sparse of gentle green leaf. The tree and the man get wet, neither cares though" (**60**,22ff.). In the early morning the police find him. "His rain has taken him away from his useless, used-up life. Perhaps back to the Dreamtime he understood. No one knew the old Wongi was dead until the next pension day" (**60**,31ff.).

The setting of this short story is Western Australia both before and after 1967, the year when the Aborigines were given the status of citizens, making them eligible to vote and to receive social service benefits. However, many of them – especially older people – were still trapped in the lowest socio-economic group of Australian society, urban and semi-urban Aborigines "who hug the dark corners and scuttle hideously from rusted hiding place to rusted hiding place" (**54**,6f.). One of these uprooted people is the old black man in Weller's "Pension Day", whose life story is told by an omniscient author. His whole life is characterised by a chain of losses. At eighteen he is deprived of the security of his tribal community with its religious and social bonds, and he loses his liberty for seven long years. Then, for a short time, he enjoys the illusion of success and acceptance in the white man's world, but with the loss of his wife he realises that he has not really escaped from his racially determined place in society. The death of his wife is the beginning of a series of losses: his house, his children, his pride, his self-respect, his physical strength and, finally, his life. His death is evocative of *Going Home*, the title of the collection which includes "Pension Day". Though in some of these stories 'home' has an ironic meaning, e.g. police custody or jail as the 'home' which white man's society has constructed for the black man, in "Pension Day" the old Wongi's death delivers him from the cold world of the white man to be taken back home, perhaps to the mythical world of his ancestors.

# Teaching Unit I

**Preparation:** Read the first 24 lines

## On pension day

### 1. Setting

*What part of Australia is the story set in and what social group does it deal with?*

The story is set in Western Australia. The old Aboriginal, a Wongi from out near Laverton, is sitting in a park in Perth, the capital of Western Australia.

*Fact-finding assignments:*

The following assignments may be dealt with by two groups of students. Using reference books and (or) the internet they should find out facts about:

**Group 1:** Western Australia (history of exploration and settlement including the towns of Perth and Laverton)

**Group 2:** The Aborigines (history, culture and religion).

### 2. The opening

*What conclusions can be drawn from the first sentence?*

The first sentence leaves no doubt that "Pension Day" is a typical short story. It starts in 'medias res', i.e. the reader is plunged into a crucial situation that is part of the related sequence of events in the life of an old black man. From the use of the definite article he/she can deduce that the narrator is about to describe an individual fate, but that probably the old man will remain unnamed throughout the story. Being "away from everyone else" (**54**,1) he has obviously been ostracized by his fellow human beings and lives totally alone. This state of isolation cannot be of a temporary nature, for instead of the continuous form of the verb, the narrator uses the simple present.

*Through whose eyes do we view the Aborigine's situation?*

As the narrator tells the story in the present tense we can deduce that he is the immediate observer, the eye-witness. From an initial position of observer-narrator "All day the black old man sits" (**54**,1) he moves to a more omniscient role. He knows that the old man wears "his black coat every day" (**54**,2) and he is informed both about the past of the coat "Once it had silver buttons ..." (**54**,2f.) and the Aborigine's past, for he had been "the leader of the redback people" (**54**,6), "a Wongi from out near Laverton" (**54**,18).

*Is the old man an individual case or does he represent a specific social or ethnic class?*
Though the definite article is suggestive of an individual case, there is no doubt that the old Wongi exemplifies the situation of his ethnic group, uprooted urban Aborigines who "hug the dark corners and scuttle hideously from rusted hiding place to rusted hiding place" (**54**,6f.).

*What role do the old man's coat and the war cannons play?*
The coat, which is old and black like the Wongi himself, reflects the life story of the Aborigine. Both suffer a parallel fate. The coat has seen better days, for it used to be a status symbol with "silver buttons and a silk collar [...] worn in the best society with speeches, silver and champagne" (**54**,2ff.), just as the old Wongi had been a respected and esteemed "leader of the redback people" (**54**,6). But both have been deprived of their original splendour and have become outcasts (or cast-offs). The war cannons, too, were "yesterday's pride" (**54**,16). However, like the old Wongi, they are discarded and disregarded by today's people who swish by in their cars "not even knowing they are there" (**54**,14f.). There is no room, neither for "yesterday's pride" nor for "yesterday's people" (**54**,16f.).

# Teaching Unit II

**Reading assignment**: While reading the whole short story the students should make notes on the different periods in the old Wongi's life.

## The life story

**1. Place the quotes and explain their significance**
- "he ... moaned in terror as the ground swept away before him" (**54**,20f.)
- "The law was the law" (**55**,2)
- "He decided to learn more about the white man's ways" (**56**,1f.)
- "He felt like a king then, a leader of the people" (**57**,2)
- "Then they all got back in their old cars and trucks and left" (**57**,28f.)
- "The next morning the boss came and got him out" (**58**,8)
- "They were all brothers now – getting drunk together" (**58**,24)
- "He smiles, uncomprehending, and nods his head" (**59**,18)
- "Everyone goes home, to wherever home is" (**60**,11)
- "His rain has taken him away" (**60**,31)

**2. Reminiscences**

*What change comes about in page 54, line 19?*

With the sudden shift from the present tense to the past tense ("When he first came ...", **54**,19) the narrator gives up his initial position of observer and the reader is offered a look into the life story of the protagonist. As an omniscient author the narrator is in control of all information, which contains not only the past events and the actions of the old Wongi, but also his innermost thoughts.

**3. Chain of events**

**Note**: In order to recall the chain of events within the chronological progression and the sequence of places, students and teacher should now make up the following diagram, determining the different stages in the old Wongi's life before analysing each stage.

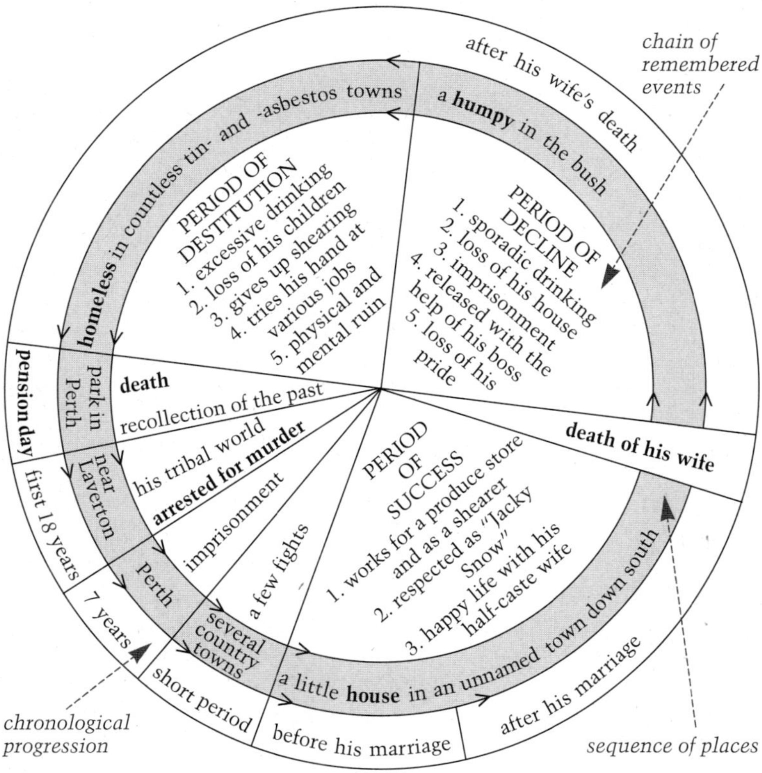

**The different stages:**
1. Being uprooted (**54**,19–**56**,2)
2. Illusion of success and acceptance in a new world (**56**,3–**57**,25)
3. Decline and destitution (**57**,26–**58**,32)

**Homework**: Each student chooses one period in the Aborigine's life and works at the tasks outlined in the next teaching unit (III), stages I to III. Later the results should be presented to the class in the chronological sequence of the stages.

## Teaching Unit III

### Stage I: Being uprooted (**54**,19–**56**,2)

**Tasks**
*1. Scan the text and mark or note down all the words, expressions, or passages that characterize the universe of the old man's youth, the sudden raid by the police and his reaction in the police Land Rover.*
**Expected solution**:
His universe: "trees and rocks and mountains" (**54**,21) – red dust (**55**,13) – "his red land's breast" (**54**,25) – "A life for a life. That was how the law had worked" (**55**,1) – "singing softly, by his campfire" (**55**,5) [= security, sense of fellowship and harmony]
Police raid: Disruption of peace and harmony – "Three policemen had sprung upon him" (**55**,3f.) – "dogs had barked and children screamed, his young girl woman ... cried" (**55**,6f.) – resignation and apathy of the old men (cf. **55**,9ff.) – "handcuffs around his great wrists" (**54**,23)
Removal: "being pushed gently into the hard, hot Land Rover" (**55**,14) – "he huddled in the back" (**54**,19f.) – "moaned in terror" (**54**,20) – "a tear slid out of his frightened, puzzled eyes" (**55**,14f.) – he "hunched into himself" (**55**,16)

*2. Analyse the 'culprit's' behaviour during and shortly after his imprisonment, choosing one typical sentence as a starting point.*
**Expected solution**:
"He had worked all day and at night he had willed himself over the walls back to his country" (**55**,23ff.)
On the one hand, the seven years of hard work in jail had neither weakened his physical strength nor his self-confidence, but on the other hand, his constant dream of home had finally given way to

reality. He knew he could never go home again, for he would be "killed […] if not by the relatives of his victim, certainly by the new husband to whom the elders would long ago have given his woman" (**55**,31ff.). He knew, too, that "white man secrets and dreams" (**55**,28f.) of profit and wealth had devastated the original character of his native land by digging "yellow-sided holes many metres deep. Black open mouths gulping in the hot air" (**55**,27f.). So he has no option but "to learn more about the white man's ways" (**56**,1f.) and live in two worlds.

## Stage II: Illusion of success and acceptance in a new world (56,3–57,25)

**Tasks**

*1. Make a table of the Wongi's personal success and his success at work in his new world.*

**Expected solution**:

| personal success | success at work |
|---|---|
| – is protected by his boss | – job in a produce store and doing some shearing |
| – marries a half-caste girl | – loves shearing and feels like a king, for the sheep obey his orders in his own language |
| – is taught a little more English | – respected by the other shearers for his size and strength |
| – is granted citizen rights | – is put on the shearing team alongside all the whites |
| – lives in a little house | – takes pride in his new position |
| – happy family life with several children | |

*2. Answer the following question:*
*Like all so-called primitive races the Aborigines respect all creatures. But 'Snowy Jackson' is cruel to sheep (cf.* **57**,*7ff.). What might be the reason for this extraordinary behaviour? Remember the role these animals have played in Australia's colonial history.*
**Expected solution**:
Unlike the white man, who traditionally regards the sheep or lamb as a symbol of gentleness and innocence, the Aborigines associate the sheep with aggressiveness. This association has its roots in their recent history, for the sheep has become a symbol of the white man's rural expansion, which was one of the main causes of their own expulsion and gradual dispossession.

*3. Describe the relationship between 'Snowy Jackson' and his "brown, sharper brethren".*
**Expected solution**:
Having grown up in the white man's world the half-castes have lost all contact with the world of their ancestors, and have adopted the mentality of the whites. Therefore, these "sharper brethren" (**56**,13) dislike the full blood's attitude to work and his close-fistedness as he refuses "to share his money around" (**56**,15). But as he evokes in them a faint recollection of the "laws and secrets" (**56**,17) of their blood relations who still live in "the shimmering emptiness of the desert" (**56**,16f.) they fear his "spiritual powers" (**56**,16) just as they live in awe of his physical strength. Even his half-caste wife, who does everything to make him familiar with the white man's language and religion, is unable to gain access to his world of the "swirling Dreaming" (**57**,20).

## Stage III: Decline and destitution (57,26–58,32)

**Tasks**
*1. Examine the meaning of 'tears' and 'rain' after the death of his wife.*
**Expected solution**:
With the sudden death of his wife 'Snowy Jackson' is deprived of the centre of his new life and has to suffer a second crucial break in his life. The tragedy of each break is marked by tears (cf. **55**,14f. and **58**,1f.). When his wife was still alive "he used to love the rain" (**57**,31) for it had been a reminder of his former natural world, a link between the world of Dreaming and the urban world pressed on him by the whites. It had given him confidence. But now with the loss of his wife his mood changes from confidence to hopelessness and despair. Therefore, he now hates the rain that turns "the sky grey and

the world cold" (**57**,30). And in his sorrow he becomes depressive and like many depressive people he seeks refuge in drinking.

*2. Scan the text and make a list of the Wongi's losses that are caused by the death of his wife.*
**Expected solution:**
Death of his wife = loss of his mainstay → Resulting losses: his confidence (→ alcohol) – his sense of responsibility – his house (**58**,3f.) – his self-control (→ temporary imprisonment) – his pride (**58**,12) – his children (**58**,16ff.) – his place in society (**58**,14f.) – his physical strength (**58**,20f.) – his permanent home (**58**,25) – his human dignity (**58**,26ff.).

# Teaching Unit IV

## Back to pension day (58,33 to the end)

### 1. The outcast and his young, black brethren

*To what extent do the young people aggravate the old black man's tragic situation ?*
The switch from the past tense to the present tense makes clear that the narrator returns to the starting point, the park in Perth on pension day. The boys "who drag lazily past" (**58**,33) are confident and optimistic about their future as they "swagger, shout and laugh loudly" (**59**,4f.). Thus they form a stark contrast to the old Aborigine who has become a human wreck,worn out by alcohol and a hard life. The "colossus" (**56**,12) has become the laughing stock of everybody. Even those who are related to him by blood (cf. black eyes – **59**,4; dark group – **59**,8; black fingers – **59**,22) sneer at him, aggravating his desperate situation. Instead of showing respect for the old man they shower him with abuse (cf. bastard – **59**,9; murderer **59**,15) and even pervert his former nickname, 'Snowy Jackson', a name synonymous with strength[1], and now call him 'Snowman' (**59**,14 + 29), probably alluding either to his looking 'snowed' (*sl.* doped or drugged) after his excessive use of alcohol or perhaps to his white hair.

---

[1] His former nickname **Jackie Snow / Snowy Jackson** was either an allusion to **Jackie Howe** (1855–1932), the Australian winner of several shearing competitions, or **Peter Jackson** (1861–1901), one of the first distinguished, black Australian professional boxers.

*How does 'Snowy Jackson' respond to their crude behaviour?*
In spite of all the insults and disrespectful behaviour the old Wongi remains totally passive, because he has lost both his mental and his physical power. He cannot beg for a cigarette, for "the wine [...] thickens his tongue" (**59**,1f.), and while being mocked at he even "smiles, uncomprehending, and nods his head" (**59**,18). He is so helpless that "they steal $ 20 from him with quick black fingers" (**59**,22).

**2. The old Wongi's catharsis – his 'going home'**
*What is the old black man's state of mind before the thunderstorm sets in?*
Dazed by "the last of his methylated spirits" (**59**,34f.) he watches the activities around him as "the tribe goes walkabout" (**60**,3) in a modern, ironical sense, wandering from group to group, drinking and fighting among themselves. Finally, "everyone goes home, to where home is" (**60**,11) but "he stays" (**60**,12) even when "the rain starts off fat and slow but becomes faster and leaner" (**60**,17).

*How does his life end?*
When "he suddenly vomits" (**60**,19) – a rather literal symbol of catharsis – he purges himself of the alcohol that has ruined his life and of the "pension day money" (**60**,19) generously granted by the white man's government. And he becomes reconciled with the rain, for it cleanses him, washing "the vomit off him, with soft hands" (**60**,26). Moreover, 'his' rain becomes his 'saviour' taking "him away from his useless, used-up life" (**60**,31). So he 'goes home' (cf. *Going Home*, the title of the collection which includes "Pension Day"), "perhaps back to the Dreamtime he understood" (**60**,31f.).

Thea Astley

# Heart is Where the Home is

## Interpretation and Teaching Notes

### Introductory Information

"Tens of thousands of Aboriginal children have been taken from their families, lied to, secreted away, stolen and placed as far away as possible, sometimes overseas, to break any links with their own community. They grew up close to the missionaries, ashamed of their aboriginality, without their language or their links to the past. That was the intention." [1]

"We need to acknowledge and accept these awful aspects of our history. The point is, it's not ancient history we're talking about, these are lived experiences of people. It's not something in the distant past that we can conveniently dismiss as being – 'Well that was the bad old days' sort of thing. It's not, this is the ongoing effects of these practices which are felt every day." [2]

Indeed, Thea Astley's short story reminds the reader of one of the most atrocious and darkest aspects of recent Australian history. However, these practices are not new, but have a long tradition starting with the first settlements on the Australian continent.

The rapid expansion of the European colonists, mainly in the north of the continent, was accompanied by serious conflicts with the Aboriginal population. It was a common practice among the white settlers to kidnap Aboriginal women and children both for economic and sexual exploitation. According to the Industrial and Reformatory School Act of 1865 the white authorities had the right to send indigenous children to missions which were declared to be industrial schools. In 1896 Archibald Meston wrote in his fact-finding report: "Boys and girls are frequently taken from their parents and their tribes, and removed far off whence they have no chance of returning; left helpless at the mercy of those who possessed them, white people responsible to no one under no supervision by any

---

[1] Garrett, Kirsten. *ABC Radio National, Background Briefing Transcript,* 11 February 1996, p. 1.

[2] Dodson, Mick. ibid. p. 1.

proper authority"[3]. He suggested to isolate the native people on reserves and his report became the basis of government policy until 1965. The Aboriginal Protection and Restriction of the Sale of Opium Act of 1897 laid the foundation of the official policy to isolate indigenous people on missions and government reserves far away from the white population. It also enabled the removal of orphaned or deserted half-caste children to an orphanage. The act was replaced by the Aboriginals Preservation and Protection Act of 1939 and authorized government officials under the control of the Director of Native Affairs to remove native Australians or displace them from one reserve to another and separate children from their mothers, respectively their families. At the same time, the Director of Native Affairs was given total control over the lives of indigenous children under 21. J.W. Bleakley, who was Chief Protector from 1913 to 1939 and Director of Native Affairs after the act of 1939, was a strong supporter of the segregation of Aborigines from non-Aboriginal people, and of the practices of the missions. The conditions in the missions and government settlements, however, were far from good. Because of malnutrition and diseases the mortality rates were very high. Bleakley's successor in office, Cornelius O'Leary (1942–1963), proposed a policy of assimilation in Queensland for the first time, and by the Aborigines and Torres Strait Islanders Act of 1965 indigenous people were theoretically allowed to care for their own children. But the Director of Native Affairs could still give orders to move people between reserves. However, the breakthrough came with the Aborigines Act and Torres Strait Islanders Act in 1971.

The compulsory removal of children from their families and the attempt of the authorities to absorb the natives into the white population had gone hand in hand with cruel methods and had had destructive consequences. Children were hunted, grabbed at random and taken away on trucks; or later they were sent on holiday with white families but never returned; and their families had no chance of finding them. In the 1920s more than 80% were girls, because on the one hand they were needed as domestic servants and on the other hand it was regarded as an adequate way of preventing them from giving birth to more indigenous babies. The situation was different after the Second World War when more boys than girls were removed for fear of increasing juvenile deliquency, with the aim of educating them and turning them into useful industrial workers.

[3] Meston, Archibald. *Report on the Aboriginals of Queensland.* Brisbane: Queensland Government, 1896, p. 4.

In many cases the consequences were disastrous. The children lost their links to their past, to their own history and culture, suffered chronic depression or became alcoholics. Others turned criminal and ended up in prison. There is no doubt that whole families were torn apart and a whole race uprooted.

Thea Astley's short story starts at the moment when a new law has been passed by the white government, saying that black children have to be brought to a white school to be taught properly. One day policemen and government officials come to an Aboriginal camp to take the children away. In great confusion, "a fearful tug-o'-war" (**63**,11), the women try to escape with their children, whereas the men remain "sullen, powerless before this new white law they'd never heard of" (**62**,5f.). However, Bidgi Mumbler's daughter-in-law, Nelly, flees into the shrubs with her baby, for she knows what will happen from earlier incidents. At a camp near Tobaccotown[4] her cousin Ruthie had lost a child and was inconsolable (cf. **63**,30ff.). At Tobaccotown the people had been discouraged and depressed, for they had known that now everything was gone. "Land. Hunting ground. River. Fish. Gone" (**63**,34). These cultural values had been substituted by the white man's world: "New god come. Old talk still about killings. The old ones remembering the killings" (**63**,35f.). A similar incident had taken place at Tinwon.

With her baby, Charley, Nelly stumbles through the rain forest following the river while the police are pursuing her. Finally, she escapes to George Laffey's farm where her father-in-law, Bidgi, had worked for a time and where she, too, had helped. Taking no notice of Mr Laffey, who is digging in the garden, she runs to the house. Mrs Laffey takes her and her baby in. When the police come Mr and Mrs Laffey present Nelly as their housegirl. Having searched the house without any success the police leave the farm reluctantly. George had hidden the baby in the loft of their bedroom with a lolly to suck. Nelly, however, is not relieved and happy, for she knows that they will "come nex time" (**69**,29). And even when the farmer promises to do the same next time and invites her to live on the farm, together with her young husband, this is no solution for Nelly, for she does not want to leave her family. The white farmer cannot understand her. But for Nelly, family is more than a husband and a child. It is: "The old men

[4] Both Tobaccotown and Tinwon are most probably fictional places, for they do not exist in the Australian post code register. According to an e-mail from the Australian Government services [client.services@abs.gov.au] these places cannot be found "but it may be possible that the names are those of farming properties or fictional place names".

old women uncles aunts cousins brothers sisters tin humpies bottles dogs dirty blankets tobacco handouts fight river trees all the tribe's remnants and wretchedness, destruction and misery" (**70**,25–28).

# Teaching Unit I

## The opening

The first teaching unit is meant to give the students the opportunity to infer from the title and the first lines of the story as much as possible about the story to come. For this purpose, the first ten lines should be read together in class.

**1. The title**
*What does the title imply?*
Astley here inverts the famous saying that "Home is where the heart is". In this context the word 'home' does not refer to a mere dwelling place but to a place or state to which one belongs and where one's affections are centred. Likewise, the 'heart', in this connection the human heart, is regarded as the centre of a person's innermost thoughts and secret feelings, his innermost being. Thus, the word is synonymous with 'soul' and 'spirit'. By inverting the saying Astley probably wants to make clear that the core of her short story is the human heart.

**2. The raid**
a) The opening technique
*How does the narrator open the story – with a 'scenic opening' or a 'zooming-in technique'?*
As the story opens 'in medias res', the reader is plunged into a crucial situation that is part of the related sequence of events, here a police raid on a black camp. This technique is comparable to the opening of a play ('scenic opening') when the curtain rises and the spectator is immediately confronted with a dramatic situation; or in films when the closed lens is directed at the scene from a short distance and the shutter is suddenly opened. Unlike the 'scenic opening' the 'zooming-in technique' often starts with a description of the historical and local background while the author gradually approaches the initial situation of the story.

b) The narrative perspective
*What is the narrator's point of view?*
From the very beginning of the story it becomes obvious that the perspective in the story is that of an omniscient third-person

narrator, for the narrator is in control of all the information, which contains not only the action but also the thoughts and feelings of many different characters. Thus, he / she knows what the women and men feel, why the police feel "lousy" (**62**,6), and what their innermost thoughts are. This means that the point of view changes several times within the story, Ruthie and Nelly, for example, giving their point of view of some incidents in their own Aboriginal, pidgin English.

c) The atmosphere

*How does the narrator create the specific atmosphere of the story?*

The calmness and routine that most probably characterize the atmosphere at the black camp after an untroubled night is suddenly interrupted by the unexpected emergence of policemen and "someone from the government" (**62**,1f.). As the black people know from experience that this bodes ill, the women are at first paralysed with terror and tongue-tied. They feel their hearts throbbing with fear. However, as soon as their maternal instinct rouses them from their initial paralysis, they burst into wailing and are seized by panic, "scattering and trying to run dragging their kids" (**62**,4). But the men's reactions are quite different. Feeling that they are helpless and "powerless before this new white law they'd never heard of" (**62**,5f.), they are "sullen" (**62**,5) and passive, watching what's going on without any resistance. The policeman feel "lousy" (**62**,6). In spite of being convinced of the rightfulness of their operation, for in their eyes the blacks are primitive beings (cf. the insulting words, "gins", "boongs", "buggers"), they feel uneasy and would have "liked the boongs to show a bit of fight" (**62**,7) so as to justify their rough behaviour.

After analysing the atmosphere created in the initial lines, the reader may rightly come to the conclusion that the tone of the whole story will be characterized on the one hand by the fear, panic and helplessness of the black people and on the other hand by the brutality, ruthlessness and determination of the government's willing executors.

# Teaching Unit II

## Reading assignment

While reading pages **62**,11 to **66**,10 the students should find suitable headings, mark typical stylistic features and make notes on:

1. The setting (taking the annotations in the Student's Book into account)
   and
2. the author's narrative technique.

## Checking the students' knowledge

The students are asked to put the following quotations into context and show their significance for the story:
- " 'We'll bring her up real good', they'd told Ruthie" (**63**,4)
- "... no men around, the men tricked out of camp." (**63**,14f.)
- " 'You'll have other baby', Nelly Mumbler comforted her" (**63**,29)
- " 'You'll be trouble,' they warned." (**64**,6f.)
- "Big surprise, eh, an they all gone thinkin tobacco, tucker, blankets" (**64**,17f.)
- "If she crossed she would only leave tracks" (**64**,30f.)
- "She'd been there, too, now and then, help washin, cleanin, ..." (**65**,12)
- "She eased the baby from Nelly's arms and put him down on the floor ..." (**66**,5f.)
- " 'George will think of something' " (**66**,10).

## The flight

### 1. The historical and geographical setting

*Determine the setting of the story.*
**Place:** The story is set in a rural area of Australia, on the banks of a river in the "rain forest" (**64**,32) of Northern Queensland (cf. annotations on 'Tobaccotown').
**Time:** As the Laffeys' son was born in 1923 (cf. annotations in the Student's Book) and is still a baby at the moment when Nelly Mumbler seeks refuge in their house ("a baby was crying in a back room and a small girl kept tugging at her mother's skirts" – **65**,24f.), we can determine the exact year of the police raid on the black camp. It takes place in the year 1923.

### 2. The narrative technique

*How does the narrator succeed in keeping the reader's suspense?*
The account of Nelly's flight is based on the alternation between the description of the successive stages of the flight and the flashbacks to past events. Thanks to this technique the narrator achieves a high degree of suspense, for the interruption of the chronological sequence of events enables the author both to avoid the monotony of chronological story-telling and to keep up the reader's suspense as to what will happen to Nelly.

| The flight | | Flashbacks |
|---|---|---|
| Nelly flees from the camp (**62**,11–**63**,1) | → | incident at Tobaccotown (**63**,1–**64**,3) |
| Nelly on the run I (**64**,4–14) | → | incident at Tinwon (**64**,15–27) |
| Nelly on the run II (**62**,28–**65**,22) | → | |
| Nelly finds refuge (**65**,23–**66**,10) | → | |

**a) The flashbacks**

*What narrative technique are the flashbacks based on and what is their purpose?*

Because of the experience of the actual raid on her camp, recollections of former, similar events at Tobaccotown and Tinwon flash through Nelly's mind and the reader can listen to her interior monologue. Thus, she provides her / him with the necessary background information on past events which explains the present situation and at the same time emphasizes the alarming proportions of the impending danger.

**Quotes providing background information**

I. The fate of the Aboriginal people in the <u>past</u>

- they have lost everything: "Land. Hunting grounds. River. Fish. Gone. New god come. Old talk still about killings. The old ones remembering the killings" (**63**,34ff.).

II. The Aborigines' <u>present</u> situation (1923)

- according to the "new white law" (**62**,5) black and half-caste children are to be separated from their parents in order to "bring [them] up real good, [...] take [them] away to big school and teach [them] proper [...] about Jesus" (**63**,4ff.).
- the black people's helplessness
  the men were "so angry they jus drank when they could get it" (**63**,32f.) and the women are "slammed into speechlessness" (**63**,7), trying in vain to save their children.

III. The government officials' <u>strategy</u>

- empty and deceitful promises
  "There was all them words, too many of them ..." (**63**,9f.); "The govmin said for them all to come long train. Big surprise, eh, an they all gone thinkin tobacco, tucker, blankets." (**64**,16ff.); "the

women they all excited waitin long that train, all the kids playin, ..." (**64**,19f.)

- precautionary measures
  the men are "tricked out of camp" (**63**,15), e.g. to "help work haulin trees up that loggin camp" (**64**,19f.)
- unconcealed brutality
  "the welfare officer with the police, all pulling, the kid howling" (**63**,12f.); "[the police] gallop after her an hit her one two, cracka cracka, with his big whip right across the face" (**63**,21f.); "two policemen they come an start grabbin, grabbin all the kids, every kid, and the kids they screamin " (**64**,20ff.); "One of the police, he got real angry and start shovin the women back hard" (**64**,23f.); "they can see the kids clutchin at the windows and some big white woman inside that train, she pull them back" (**64**,25ff.).

**b) The course of the flight**

*Is Nelly's attempt to escape promising?*
From the very beginning the reader is almost convinced that her attempt to escape is bound to fail considering that she is confronted with the full authority of the government. Former events at Tobaccotown and Tinwon have taught her that such an attempt is futile, and she feels that her "skinny legs [don't] seem to move fast enough across that world of the policeman's eye" (**62**,12f.).

*Why is Nelly's flight successful contrary to all expectations?*
Both her character and her maternal instinct enable her to flee successfully. Unlike the other women who are "scared, fixed to the spot like they grew there, all shakin and whimperin. Stuck" (**64**,5f.), Nelly takes resolute action. Casting the other women's warnings ("you'll be trouble" – **64**,6) to the wind ("Don't care ... They not takin my kid" – **64**,8) she grabs her little boy and flees "through the scrub patch towards the river" (**62**,12). So she turns out to be a determined and courageous young woman. This disposition is supported by her closeness to nature, which is typical of all so-called primitive races. Instinctively, she flees into "the thickest part of the rain forest, following the river, well away from the track up near the packers'road" (**64**,9ff.) and when she comes to a sand strip running "half way across the river" (**64**,30) she knows that it is no use crossing here, for there is "no time to scrape away telltale footprints" (**64**,31f.). In spite of being panic-stricken she makes the right decisions.

*What makes Nelly's flight so atmospheric?*
The description of the flight is highly atmospheric for the reader's suspense is increased by constant variations of tension. There are alternations between periods of hasty flight (cf. the verbs used: to

grab – **62**,11; to worm into – **64**,9; to stumble through – **64**,11; to dodge through – **64**,28) and moments of rest, e.g. when she huddles under a bush to comfort the baby "with her nipples for a while" (**65**,2) or when she stands "uncertain by the fence" (**65**,14) of George Laffey's place. On the other hand, the distant sounds, "the yells of the women back at the camp" (**64**,29), the shouts that wind "through the forest" (**65**,4) or the wailing that filters through the trees (cf. **65**,5) make her confident that she is actually escaping, whereas her own "panting and gasping" (**64**,29), the baby's "howls" (**64**,33) and the sudden yelping of a dog "too close" (**65**,6) to her hiding place jeopardize her success. Again, she plucks up courage, pulls "herself to her feet" (**65**,6), staggers "along the sandy track" (**65**,7), thrusts "between claws of branch and thorn" (**65**,8f.), "thrusts her baby under the wire" (**65**,15), wriggles "through after him" (**65**,15), grabs the baby, "stumbles through the cow paddock" (**65**,17), and, finally, gasps past Mr Laffey "round the side of the house" (**65**,21f.). At last at the Laffey's place another period of rest begins.

**c) Stylistic features**
*What are the most noticeable features of the author's style?*
The author's style is marked by the use of a variety of figurative expressions. Thus, the women's first reaction to the raid is characterized by "the wordless terror of heart-jump" (**62**,3), Ruthie was "slammed into speechlessness" (**63**,7), and her screeching "opened up the sky and pulled it down on her" (**63**,17f.). The area that can be surveyed by the police is "the world of the policeman's eye" (**62**,13), the fight for the children is compared to "a fearful tug-o`-war" (**63**,11), the footprints that may reveal the escape route are "telltale footprints" (**64**,32) and the wailing of the women far away at the camp is "filtered through the canopy" (**65**,5). Moreover, the vividness of the language is intensified by the use of similes and onomatopoeia. The men`s rage burns "like scrub fire" (**63**,33) and the distant shouts wind "through the forest like vines" (**65**,4). Finally, when the policeman hits Ruthie with his whip across the face the sound is imitated by the onomatopoeic use of the words "cracka cracka" (**63**,21f.).

# Teaching Unit III

## Reading assignment

Read the story to the end and make notes on:
- Mag Laffey's behaviour before and after the arrival of the police
- Nelly's decision on the Laffeys' enticing offer.

## Confrontation and conflict

### 1. Reaching a safe haven

*Why can Nelly feel safe at the Laffeys' place?*

As soon as Nelly has arrived at the farm she knows that these white people are favourably disposed towards her and her people. Unlike the white government officials, the Laffeys treat her like a friend, and the first contact between their child and Nelly's Aboriginal baby, Charley, is a striking proof of a lack of prejudice, for "the children stared then reached out to touch each other" (**66**,6f.) and Mag, "watching with a smile" (**66**,6), proves to be a loving mother. Indeed, she is an understanding and good-hearted woman who does everything to calm Nelly down by her "soft" (**65**,26) speech and her soothing maternal behaviour: "Still, now [...] Tell me, Nelly. You tell me what's the matter" (**65**,30ff.). Moreover, she is a hospitable woman, pulling the black woman "gently, gently" (**65**,27) in and, finally, handing her a cup of tea. And there is no reason why Nelly should not give credence to Mag's promise that "George will think of something" (**66**,10), i.e. find a way out. However, the reader feels that this period of rest and recovery at the Laffeys' is probably no more than the calm before the storm.

### 2. The individual versus government authority

a) Uncertain chances of success

*What are the Laffeys' and Nelly's prospects when the police turn up?*

When the policemen turn up the reader is quite sure that the Laffeys will hardly be able to avert the impending danger. On the one hand, there is the awe-inspiring, macho behaviour of the police whom George watches riding "at an aggressive trot" (**66**,12f.) towards the farmhouse and then "boot-thumping up the steps" (**66**,20). On the other hand, there are Mr Laffey who goes "blank" when "confronted with their questions" (**66**,15) and his wife, Mag, whose obvious gentleness and kindness to Nelly do not seem to be promising when confronted with men whose ego is inflated by the authority invested in their office.

b) The battle for the child

*How can the Laffeys successfully protect Nelly and her son contrary to all expectations?*

The policemen's macho bearing collapses as soon as Mag "forestalled them" (**66**,21) and memories of former "brushes with George Laffey's wife" (**66**,24f.) flash through their minds. They dislike her being so inappropriately self-confident, "never [knowing] her place", but "always airing an idea of some sort" (**66**,25f.), in short "a town girl with town notions" (**66**,29). Indeed, the reader discovers a completely new side to her character, for besides her maternal kindness she is also an intrepid and determined woman. Thus "her whole body [is] a challenge" (**66**,21f.) when she first faces the policemen, and her responses to their questioning reveal a shrewd, quick-witted, and even cheeky woman, who not only criticizes the government for wasting people's time (cf. **67**,17f.) but also makes a fool of the policemen by reducing their search for "abo kids" (**66**,31) to absurdity (cf. **66**,35f.) and turning their rude criticism of Nelly's muteness ("Cat got your tongue?" – **67**,29) into a derisive attack on their own stupidity ("Perhaps the cat has your ears as well" – **67**,32). During the interrogation by the police her husband plays a more passive role, confining himself to "nodding her on" (**67**,16) and "smiling his support" (**67**,35f.) while his eyes are "strained with affection and concern" (**68**,6).

*How do the policemen behave?*
These government officials prove to be two-faced. When they are confronted with Mag, who is on a par with them, they "fidget" (**66**,24) are nervous and embarrassed (cf. **67**,1f.) and, finally, give up reluctantly. However, they treat Nelly, who is 'only' a black woman, without any respect whatsoever. Moreover, they call her and her people "Fuckin' boongs" (**69**,4), and when they start searching the house, they flatten "Nelly Mumbler against the wall" (**68**,12f.).

### 3. Resisting temptation

a) Nelly's dilemma

*What is Nelly's situation after the danger has been averted?*
Just as we feel that disaster has been averted, Nelly is in a quandary when George invites her to live on the farm together with her child and her husband, so as to prevent them from being separated from their baby.

The following diagram of Nelly's dilemma should appear on the board:

**Nelly**

| living at the Laffeys': | living at the black camp: |
|---|---|
| 1. economic security | 1. poverty |
| 2. (comparative) security for her son | 2. danger for her son |
| 3. pleasant, friendly surroundings | 3. wretched surroundings |
| 4. protected by white family | 4. among her own extended family (tribe) |

b) George's proposal
*What is George aiming at when making his offer? Why does he get so annoyed with Nelly? Discuss.*
This time it is George who takes the initiative. Picking up "the small black boy and his daughter and [...] bouncing a child on each knee, waggling his head lovingly between them both while small hands pawed his face" (**69**,24ff.), he makes the impression of a loving father and a caring person. But when Nelly does not accept his offer of accommodation, he becomes "exasperated" (**70**,8) as he really cannot understand why she rejects his offer of comparative security and clean housing for the wretched camp. He loses patience with her and cries "from the depth of his understanding" (**70**,15), revealing the cultural gulf between the two of them. Nevertheless, we must presume that his offer of accommodation is genuine and that he is not just thinking of gaining cheap black help.

c) The limits of white paternalism
*Why does Nelly refuse the security offered by the Laffeys?*
George (and perhaps his wife too) cannot understand why Nelly will not leave the black camp and live with them in order to protect her child from being taken away by the authorities. This lack of understanding is caused by the white man's ignorance of the heart and soul of Aboriginals and their cultural values. For these people, a family is far more than parents and children. It is the extended family, the familiar atmosphere of the black camp, their closeness to nature and the fate of their race including "wretchedness, destruction and misery" (**70**,27f.). Now the reader remembers the title of the short story : "Heart is Where the Home is".

## Post-reading activity

The students (individuals, pairs, or groups) are asked to check all the reference books which are available to them or use the internet (www.qld.gov.au) for facts about Queensland with special regard to the following aspects:

*1. The geographical character of Queensland including its specific flora and fauna.*

*2. The history of Queensland, including that of the Aboriginal population, the early exploration and white colonization.*